OPPOSING
VIEWPOINTS®
SERIES

| Party Politics

Other Books of Related Interest

Opposing Viewpoints Series

Campaign Finance
Identity Politics
Politics and Journalism in a Post-Truth World
Western Democracy at Risk

At Issue Series

Gerrymandering and Voting Districts
Political Corruption
Politicians on Social Media
The Role of Religion in Public Policy

Current Controversies Series

Interference in Elections
The Political Elite and Special Interests
Political Extremism in the United States
The Two-Party System in the United States

"Congress shall make
no law ... abridging
the freedom of speech,
or of the press."

First Amendment to the US Constitution

The basic foundation of our democracy is the First Amendment guarantee of freedom of expression. The Opposing Viewpoints series is dedicated to the concept of this basic freedom and the idea that it is more important to practice it than to enshrine it.

OPPOSING
VIEWPOINTS®
SERIES

| Party Politics

Avery Elizabeth Hurt, Book Editor

GREENHAVEN
PUBLISHING

Published in 2021 by Greenhaven Publishing, LLC
353 3rd Avenue, Suite 255, New York, NY 10010

First Edition

Cover image: cowardlion/Shutterstock.com

Library of Congress Cataloging-in-Publication Data

Names: Hurt, Avery Elizabeth, editor.
Title: Party politics / Avery Elizabeth Hurt, book editor.
Other titles: Party politics (Greenhaven Publishing)
Description: First edition. | New York : Greenhaven Publishing, 2021. |
  Series: Opposing viewpoints | Includes bibliographical references and
  index. | Audience: Grades 9–12
Identifiers: LCCN 2019057569 | ISBN 9781534506855 (library binding) | ISBN
  9781534506848 (paperback)
Subjects: LCSH: Political parties—United States—Juvenile literature. |
  Political culture—United States—Juvenile literature. | Political
  corruption—United States—Juvenile literature. | Polarization (Social
  sciences)—Political aspects—United States—Juvenile literature.
Classification: LCC JK2265 .P36 2021 | DDC 324.273—dc23
LC record available at https://lccn.loc.gov/2019057569

Manufactured in the United States of America

Website: http://greenhavenpublishing.com

Contents

Chapter 3: Would the United States Benefit from a Multi-Party Political System?

Chapter 4: Can the United States Transcend Party Politics?

The Importance of Opposing Viewpoints

Perhaps every generation experiences a period in time in which the populace seems especially polarized, starkly divided on the important issues of the day and gravitating toward the far ends of the political spectrum and away from a consensus-facilitating middle ground. The world that today's students are growing up in and that they will soon enter into as active and engaged citizens is deeply fragmented in just this way. Issues relating to terrorism, immigration, women's rights, minority rights, race relations, health care, taxation, wealth and poverty, the environment, policing, military intervention, the proper role of government—in some ways, perennial issues that are freshly and uniquely urgent and vital with each new generation—are currently roiling the world.

If we are to foster a knowledgeable, responsible, active, and engaged citizenry among today's youth, we must provide them with the intellectual, interpretive, and critical-thinking tools and experience necessary to make sense of the world around them and of the all-important debates and arguments that inform it. After all, the outcome of these debates will in large measure determine the future course, prospects, and outcomes of the world and its peoples, particularly its youth. If they are to become successful members of society and productive and informed citizens, students need to learn how to evaluate the strengths and weaknesses of someone else's arguments, how to sift fact from opinion and fallacy, and how to test the relative merits and validity of their own opinions against the known facts and the best possible available information. The landmark series Opposing Viewpoints has been providing students with just such critical-thinking skills and exposure to the debates surrounding society's most urgent contemporary issues for many years, and it continues to serve this essential role with undiminished commitment, care, and rigor.

The key to the series' success in achieving its goal of sharpening students' critical-thinking and analytic skills resides in its title—

Opposing Viewpoints. In every intriguing, compelling, and engaging volume of this series, readers are presented with the widest possible spectrum of distinct viewpoints, expert opinions, and informed argumentation and commentary, supplied by some of today's leading academics, thinkers, analysts, politicians, policy makers, economists, activists, change agents, and advocates. Every opinion and argument anthologized here is presented objectively and accorded respect. There is no editorializing in any introductory text or in the arrangement and order of the pieces. No piece is included as a "straw man," an easy ideological target for cheap point-scoring. As wide and inclusive a range of viewpoints as possible is offered, with no privileging of one particular political ideology or cultural perspective over another. It is left to each individual reader to evaluate the relative merits of each argument—as he or she sees it, and with the use of ever-growing critical-thinking skills—and grapple with his or her own assumptions, beliefs, and perspectives to determine how convincing or successful any given argument is and how the reader's own stance on the issue may be modified or altered in response to it.

This process is facilitated and supported by volume, chapter, and selection introductions that provide readers with the essential context they need to begin engaging with the spotlighted issues, with the debates surrounding them, and with their own perhaps shifting or nascent opinions on them. In addition, guided reading and discussion questions encourage readers to determine the authors' point of view and purpose, interrogate and analyze the various arguments and their rhetoric and structure, evaluate the arguments' strengths and weaknesses, test their claims against available facts and evidence, judge the validity of the reasoning, and bring into clearer, sharper focus the reader's own beliefs and conclusions and how they may differ from or align with those in the collection or those of their classmates.

Research has shown that reading comprehension skills improve dramatically when students are provided with compelling, intriguing, and relevant "discussable" texts. The subject matter of these collections could not be more compelling, intriguing, or urgently relevant to today's students and the world they are poised to inherit. The anthologized articles and the reading and discussion questions that are included with them also provide the basis for stimulating, lively, and passionate classroom debates. Students who are compelled to anticipate objections to their own argument and identify the flaws in those of an opponent read more carefully, think more critically, and steep themselves in relevant context, facts, and information more thoroughly. In short, using discussable text of the kind provided by every single volume in the Opposing Viewpoints series encourages close reading, facilitates reading comprehension, fosters research, strengthens critical thinking, and greatly enlivens and energizes classroom discussion and participation. The entire learning process is deepened, extended, and strengthened.

For all of these reasons, Opposing Viewpoints continues to be exactly the right resource at exactly the right time—when we most need to provide readers with the critical-thinking tools and skills that will not only serve them well in school but also in their careers and their daily lives as decision-making family members, community members, and citizens. This series encourages respectful engagement with and analysis of opposing viewpoints and fosters a resulting increase in the strength and rigor of one's own opinions and stances. As such, it helps make readers "future ready," and that readiness will pay rich dividends for the readers themselves, for the citizenry, for our society, and for the world at large.

Introduction

> "*However [political parties] may now
> and then answer popular ends, they
> are likely in the course of time and
> things, to become potent engines,
> by which cunning, ambitious, and
> unprincipled men will be enabled to
> subvert the power of the people and
> to usurp for themselves the reins of
> government, destroying afterwards
> the very engines which have lifted
> them to unjust dominion.*"

> —*George Washington,
> Farewell Address*

Whether you regularly follow politics or watch election returns only one evening every fourth November, you may have gotten the impression that the whole US political party system is like a big sporting match. Team Blue (the Democrats) and Team Red (the Republicans) compete for the big prize: the presidency or control of one or both houses of Congress. If you're a serious politics nerd, you closely follow state races as well. (You may even be the rare bird who keeps up with local politics. If so, good for you!) But even to the dedicated and informed, the entire political enterprise can resemble entertainment more than government. The winning team gets bragging rights for four (or two, depending on the race) years. The losers become the not-so-loyal opposition, biding their time and crafting their strategy for the next election.

Of course, there is a great deal more at stake. But with the way party politics plays out in the United States these days, it can be easy to lose sight of that. We often forget that the point of winning elections is to govern once in office. As soon as officials are elected, they become public servants. The point of a representative democracy is that the people elect leaders who in turn work for the interests of the public—even the public who didn't vote for them.

Don't Bet Against This Country

For the most part, the founding fathers didn't approve of political parties. Alexander Hamilton called them the "fatal disease" of popular governments. In *The Federalist Papers*, James Madison, who was the primary architect of the US Constitution, warned of the "violence of factions." (*Factions* was the word the founders used for parties.)

There were exceptions. Thomas Jefferson seemed to approve of political parties, or at least thought they were inevitable, humans being what they are. Perhaps because Jefferson didn't play much of a role in drafting the Constitution, there is no mention of parties in it.

Because the Constitution offered no guidance, political parties have developed on their own, changing with the times and playing an important, though not well-defined role in the American political system.

Though many Americans are quite wedded to their parties, polls show that a majority would prefer more choices. Some studies have found that as many as two-thirds of voters think the US needs a third party. Yet they're not likely to get one anytime soon. The winner-take-all system of US elections almost guarantees the dominance of two major parties. Other parties—the Green Party, Libertarians, Democratic Socialists, and several others—are increasingly active and can have an influence on public discourse. However, they have little to no chance of winning major elections. That leaves the country trapped in a two-party system, despite the fact than many people see it as increasingly dysfunctional and sometimes even corrupt.

Today, George Washington's fears, as expressed in the quotation above, seem well justified. However, there is a great deal of disagreement about just what the problem is. There is even more variation in views about how to fix the broken system.

This volume's viewpoints reflect that. Some authors think the US must figure out a way to make a multi-party system work. Others think the two-party system is the more stable arrangement and needs only to be strengthened and possibly repaired. Some say the solution is more citizen involvement—better voter turnout, more grassroots action. One author suggests ballot initiatives as a way to transcend party politics.

America's fractious political parties and fractured political landscape pose a complex problem that resists simple answers. However, the United States has a history of rebounding from adversity. In 2019, American journalist Michael Lewis told the *Guardian*, "My gut says don't bet against the country. [The US] has this incredible capacity for self-reinvention."

Party politics is an interesting topic for a volume in the Opposing Viewpoints series. Our party system is a classic example of opposing viewpoints. The articles featured here represent many varied and often opposing views. Yet interestingly, they do not present a starkly divided landscape of right and left, blue and red, Democrat and Republican. In chapters titled "What Purpose Do Political Parties Serve in the United States?" "Do Political Parties Encourage Corruption?" "Would the United States Benefit from a Multi-Party Political System?" and "Can the United States Transcend Party Politics?" the viewpoints in *Opposing Viewpoints: Party Politics* highlight the complexity of the issue, but they also show how viewing the problem from a variety of perspectives is likely to lead to more fruitful discussions and potential solutions— not just one solution, but a constellation of them. It's as if the extremity of the opposing viewpoints has forced careful, caring thinkers to seek common ground and workable solutions.

OPPOSING
VIEWPOINTS®
SERIES

CHAPTER 1

What Purpose Do Political Parties Serve in the United States?

Chapter Preface

In the United States, political parties have been around since the nation's birth, though their names have changed and their priorities have shifted throughout the years. Nonetheless, the basic role of political parties is much as it always was. Parties provide a means for like-minded voters to organize to have their voices heard and their concerns addressed. They select, train, and support candidates for political office. They then hold those candidates to policy positions supported by party members and party supporters (which are not completely overlapping groups).

By selecting and supporting candidates for office (at the local, state, and national levels) political parties also serve the purpose of narrowing the choices for voters. A voter who is aligned with the basic policy positions of a given party can confidently select a candidate from that party knowing that he or she will, in most cases, represent their interests reasonably well once in office. Thanks to the United States' strongly entrenched two-party system, voters have little choice but to choose a party and vote for its candidates—and if those candidates are to have any chance of winning an election, they must be aligned with one of the major parties, Republican or Democratic.

Yet in modern times the two major US political parties do not always seem to function very smoothly or to serve the body politic as well as they should. Parties often pander to the most extreme elements in their parties. This had led to an alarming amount of distance between the positions of the two major parties—so much distance, in fact, that they no longer seem to be able to work together for the common good. But as with most issues, what led to this point, how dangerous it really is, and what, if anything, should be done about it, is a complex issue. In the viewpoints that follow, you will read about the causes and effects of political polarization and why it might not be as bad as some people think.

> *"Political parties occupy a vague space in the U.S. as semi-public organizations that have private interests but play important public roles."*

Political Parties Play a Powerful Role in the American Political System

Tom Murse

In the following viewpoint, Tom Murse provides a succinct overview of what political parties are, what they do, and how they came into being. Murse discusses political parties at the local, state, and national level. He also examines the positions of the major US parties, Democratic and Republican, as well as the positions of the Green, Libertarian, and Constitution parties. Tom Murse is a veteran political reporter and editor of the LNP, *a daily newspaper in Lancaster, Pennsylvania.*

As you read, consider the following questions:

1. What is the distinction between being a member of a party and being affiliated with that party?
2. What does the author mean when he describes political parties as occupying a "vague space" in the United States?
3. Do you see any overlap among the positions of the parties?

A political party is an organized body of like-minded people who work to elect candidates for public office who represent their values on matters of policy. In the U.S., home to a strong two-party system, the major political parties are the Republicans and the Democrats. But there are many other smaller and less well organized political parties that also nominate candidates for public office; among the most prominent of these are the Green Party, the Libertarian Party, and the Constitution Party, all three of which have run candidates for president in modern elections. Still, only Republicans and Democrats have served in the White House since 1852.

The Role of a Political Party

Political parties are neither corporations nor political-action committees, nor super PACs. Nor are they nonprofit groups or charitable organizations. In fact, political parties occupy a vague space in the U.S.—as semi-public organizations that have private interests (getting their candidate elected to office) but play important public roles. Those roles include running primaries in which voters nominate candidates for local, state and federal offices, and also hosting elected party members at presidential nominating conventions every four years. In the U.S., the Republican National Committee and the Democratic National Committee are the semi-public organizations that manage the nation's two major political parties.

Am I a Member of a Political Party?

Technically, no, not unless you're elected to a local, state or federal party committee. If you're registered to vote as a Republican, Democrat or Libertarian, that means you are affiliated with a particular party and its beliefs. But you're not actually a party member.

What Political Parties Do

The primary functions of every political party are to recruit, evaluate, and nominate candidates for election at the local, state, and federal levels; to serve as opposition to the opposing political party; to draft and approve a party platform to which candidates typically must abide; and to raise large sums of money to support their candidates. The two major political parties in the U.S. raise millions of dollars each, money they spend trying to get their nominees into office.

Let's take a closer look at how political parties actually work to accomplish these goals.

Political Parties at the Local Level

Political "party committees" operate in cities, suburbs, and rural areas to find people to run for offices such as mayor, municipal governing bodies, public-school boards, and Legislature. They also evaluate candidates and offer endorsements, which serve as guidance to voters of that party. These local parties are made up of rank-and-file committee people who are, in many states, elected by voters in primaries. The local parties are, in many locations, authorized by states to provide election judges, observers and inspectors to work at polling places. Judges of elections explain voting procedures and use of voting equipment, provide ballots and monitor elections; inspectors keep an eye on the voting equipment to make sure it works properly; observers scrutinize how ballots are handled and counted to ensure accuracy. This is the fundamental public role of political parties.

Political Parties at the State Level

Political parties are made up of elected committee members, who meet to endorse candidates for governor and statewide "row offices" including attorney, treasurer, and auditor general. State political parties also help to manage the local committees and play a crucial role in mobilizing the electorate—getting voters to the polls, coordinating campaign activities such as phone banks and canvassing, and making sure all the candidates on the party ticket, from top to bottom, are consistent in their platforms and messages.

Political Parties at the National Level
The national committees set the broad agendas and platforms for the party workers at the federal, state, and local levels. The national committees, too, are made up of elected committee members. They set election strategy and organize the presidential conventions every four years, where delegates from each state gather to cast ballots and nominate candidates for president.

How Political Parties Came Into Being
The first political parties—the Federalists and the anti-Federalists—emerged from the debate over ratification of the U.S. Constitution in 1787. The formation of the second party further illustrates one of the primary functions of political parties: serving as opposition to another faction with diametrically opposed values. In this particular case, the Federalists were arguing for a strong central government and the opposing Anti-Federalists wanted the states to hold more power. The Democratic-Republicans followed soon after, founded by Thomas Jefferson and James Madison to oppose the Federalists. Then came Democrats and the Whigs.

No third-party candidate has ever been elected to the White House in modern history, and very few have won seats in either the House of Representatives or the U.S. Senate. The most notable exception to the two party system is U.S. Sen. Bernie Sanders of Vermont, a socialist whose campaign for the 2016 Democratic presidential nomination invigorated liberal members of the party. The closest any independent presidential candidate has come to being elected to the White House was billionaire Texan Ross Perot, who won 19 percent of the popular vote in the 1992 election.

List of Political Parties

The Federalists and the Whigs and the Democratic-Republicans have been extinct since the 1800s, but there are plenty of other political parties around today. Here are some of them, and the positions that make them unique:

- Republican: Takes more conservative positions on fiscal issues such as spending and the national debate and social issues such as gay marriage and abortion, both of which a majority of the party opposes. Republicans are more resistant to change in public policy than other parties.
- Democrat: Tends to favor an expansion of social programs that assist the poor, broadening coverage of government-sponsored health care, and strengthening public education systems in the U.S. Most Democrats also support the right of women to have abortions and of same-sex couples to marry, polls show.
- Libertarian: Favors a dramatic reduction in government functions, taxation and regulation and takes a hands-off approach to social issues such as drug use, prostitution, and abortion. Favors as little government intrusion into personal freedoms as possible. Libertarians tend to be fiscally conservative and liberal on social issues.
- Green: Promotes environmentalism, social justice and the rights of lesbian, gay, bisexual and transgender Americans to receive the same civil liberties and rights others enjoy. Party members typically oppose war. The party tends to be liberal on fiscal and social issues.
- Constitution: Formed as the Taxpayers Party in 1992, this party is socially and fiscally conservative. It believes the two major parties, the Republicans and Democrats, have expanded government beyond the powers granted in Constitution. In that way it is much like the Libertarian Party. However, the Constitution Party opposes abortion and same-sex marriage. It also opposes amnesty for immigrants living in the U.S. illegally, wants to disband the Federal Reserve and return to the gold standard.

"Parties don't hire, contact, or educate many young people or offer them paths to leadership."

The Influence of Political Parties Is Weaker with Millennials

Peter Levine

In the following viewpoint Peter Levine explores evidence suggesting that US millennials are not as likely as previous generations to identify with a political party. Most people who claim to be independents vote consistently with one party or another. However, Levine points out that this still has an effect on the viability of political parties. This viewpoint was written before the 2016 presidential election and draws on examples from the presidential campaigns of Bernie Sanders and Hillary Clinton. Peter Levine is associate dean for research and Lincoln Filene Professor of Citizenship & Public Affairs at Tufts University.

As you read, consider the following questions:

1. Why, according to Levine, might Bernie Sanders's status as an outsider actually increases his appeal with young voters?
2. How have political parties changed "for the worse," according to this viewpoint?
3. Levine says that parties were not responsible for the increase in youth engagement in the Sanders and Obama campaigns? What was?

Young Americans don't care much for political parties. According to the Pew Research Center, 48 percent of millennials (ages 18-33) identify as independents. That's almost as many as identify as Democrats (28 percent) and Republicans (18 percent) put together.

Political scientists are often skeptical about the independent option in surveys. Most individuals who choose to call themselves "independents" still vote consistently with one party or the other. They are partisans except in name.

Even if that's true, the lack of loyalty or concern for parties still has consequences. For instance, presidential primary campaigns were established to allow a party's members to choose its candidate. But the research team at Tufts University's Tisch College, where I study civic engagement, estimates that young Americans (18-30) have so far cast more votes for Senator Bernie Sanders than for Secretary Hillary Clinton and Donald Trump combined.

Sanders is a party outsider. He ran all his previous campaigns as a socialist, defeating Democrats on the way to statewide office. His career outside the Democratic Party doesn't faze young Democratic primary voters—and I suspect it even increases his appeal with youth.

Does the fact that young people ignore or dislike parties tell us something about youth and their culture, or is this more about the parties and how they have changed?

THE US POLITICAL SYSTEM IS MORE DIVIDED THAN EVER

Party polarization is even worse than most people think, according to a new Michigan State University study.

And neither party can shoulder the blame, as it doesn't matter which party is in charge, said Zachary Neal, associate professor of psychology and global urban studies.

"What I've found is that polarization has been steadily getting worse since the early 1970s," he said. "Today, we've hit the ceiling on polarization. At these levels, it will be difficult to make any progress on social or economic policies."

In one of the first studies to address polarization not only in terms of who works together, but also who doesn't, Neal analyzed publicly available data on who sponsors bills in Congress from 1973 to 2016. He specifically looked at how often politicians from both sides of the aisle co-sponsor legislation.

Published in the journal Social Networks, the study found although thousands of bills are introduced each year, the average representative or senator co-sponsors only about 200. And when they decide with whom to co-sponsor bills, they view nearly half of their colleagues as "the opposition."

Rejecting the Hierarchy

Today's young voters have grown up in an age of social media. Millennials both expect and prefer loose networks that allow individuals to personalize their views and form and shift relationships freely. That's bad news for political parties—hierarchical organizations with officers, rules, official platforms and membership criteria.

Religion offers a parallel case. The pollster Anna Greenberg finds that young Americans are still spiritual—indeed, they continue to believe in many traditional tenets of religion—but they are not drawn to traditional religious institutions. She argues that young people expect to be able to choose exactly the religious

While it's hard to imagine incivility among Democrats and Republicans getting worse, it likely will, Neal said, especially if one party barely holds the majority.

The Affordable Care Act is an example, Neal said. The Democrats held a slim majority—just enough to get the bill passed. Then the Republicans took control, again with a slim majority, and tried to repeal it.

"We're seeing lots of animosity in politics," he said. "Although bills do occasionally get passed, they don't stick around long enough, or never get fully implemented, and therefore don't have lasting impact. This kind of partisanship means that our democracy has reached a kind of stalemate."

So, what's the solution?

It could be electing more centrists to Congress, Neal said. But that'll be tough because centrists often don't appeal to American voters, who are increasingly polarized too.

"This study raises new questions about the future of Congressional politics," he said. "In truth, the only thing that is bi-partisan in Congress is the trend toward greater polarization."

"Republican Divide Is Worst It's Ever Been," by Kristen Parker and Zachary Neal, Michigan State University, October 1, 2018.

content they prefer and to express their individual preferences in much the same way as they choose music and consumer goods.

It is hard for a political party to offer such personalization, because it must promote a platform. In contrast, loosely organized social movements like Black Lives Matter or Spain's Los Indignados (anti-austerity protesters) allow participants to express their personal views and to connect to the peers they most like within the movement.

I acknowledge that this cultural shift is part of the story, but I don't think it alone explains the decline of parties. For one thing, social media is just as important in Europe as it is in North America, but according to the European Social Survey (ESS), young Europeans' trust in parties has risen and surpasses that of older Europeans.

Los Indignados began as a decentralized online social movement but has morphed into a political party, Podemos, that holds the third-largest number of seats in the Spanish parliament. I wouldn't say that European youth love parties, but they support the parties that reflect their views.

Parties Are Changing, Too

The theory that young Americans are deserting parties because of shifts in culture and values overlooks the fact that American political parties are changing, and mostly for the worse.

Parties used to raise a lot of money and spend it to employ grassroots workers, recruit volunteers, choose and constrain candidates, generate consistent messages, drive policy agendas, and control patronage jobs. That system involved corruption, which was a good reason to reform it. But after the campaign finance reforms of the 1970s had restricted the parties' ability to raise and spend money, the Supreme Court allowed candidates and outside entities to spend as much as they want.

As a result, the parties now do very little. They are best described as brand names for loosely connected networks of entrepreneurial candidates, donors, and advocacy organizations. Ironically, they have become more like social networks, albeit lubricated by money. The Koch brothers' political network, for instance, employs 3.5 times as many people as the Republican National Committee does.

This means that parties don't hire, contact, or educate many young people or offer them paths to leadership. Candidates and campaigns affiliated with parties may do those things, but young people still lack any contact with the party itself.

In 2004, political scientist Dan Shea surveyed local party leaders. "Only a handful" ran any "programs that require[d] a significant amount of time or resources." He also asked county leaders an open-ended question: "Are there demographic groups of voters that are currently important to the long term success of your local party?" Just eight percent named young voters.

Parties were already weak then. Youth turnout reached its nadir in 1996-2000. Since then, candidates like Obama in 2008 and Sanders in 2016 have engaged a lot of young people. Youth turnout rose, as did the proportion of young Americans who said they had been contacted by candidates. But the parties weren't doing this outreach. According to the General Social Survey, fewer than one in 10 young adults actively participated in a party in 2004, and that proportion fell to one in 40 by 2014.

We can debate whether it would be desirable, constitutional or even possible to restore the parties' importance, but as long as they don't do much for young people, young people will naturally learn to ignore them.

> *"If the opposition returns the bitter rhetoric with similar political hardball and demonizing language, they risk locking in place a cycle that leads to entrenching the politics of polarization."*

Political Polarization Damages Democracy

Jennifer Lynn McCoy

In the following viewpoint, first published just before the 2018 mid-term elections, Jennifer Lynn McCoy takes a hard look at the effects of extreme polarization on American democracy. Based on the author's research on political polarization in several other countries as well as the United States, she offers insight into what leads to polarization as well as what citizens can do to mitigate its effects. Jennifer Lynn McCoy, PhD, is Distinguished University Professor of Political Science and founding director of the Global Studies Institute at Georgia State University.

"Extreme Political Polarization Weakens Democracy—Can the US Avoid That Fate?" by Jennifer Lynn McCoy, The Conversation, October 31, 2018. https://theconversation.com/extreme-political-polarization-weakens-democracy-can-the-us-avoid-that-fate-105540.

As you read, consider the following questions:

1. What makes followers of a political group willing to tolerate undemocratic actions by leaders of that group, according to the author?
2. How has social media exacerbated this problem according to this viewpoint?
3. Why is participating in democracy—particularly in elections—the best way to reduce polarization?

T he midterm elections are approaching during one of the most polarized moments in recent American politics.

A collaborative research project I led on polarized democracies around the world examines the processes by which societies divide into political "tribes" and democracy is harmed.

Based on a study of 11 countries including the U.S., Turkey, Hungary, Venezuela, Thailand and others, we found that when political leaders cast their opponents as immoral or corrupt, they create "us" and "them" camps—called by political scientists and psychologists "in-groups" and "out-groups"—in the society.

In this tribal dynamic, each side views the other "out group" party with increasing distrust, bias and enmity.

Perceptions that "If you win, I lose" grow. Each side views the other political party and their supporters as a threat to the nation or their way of life if that other political party is in power.

For that reason, the incumbent's followers tolerate more illiberal and increasingly authoritarian behavior to stay in power, while the opponents are more and more willing to resort to undemocratic means to remove them from power.

This damages democracy.

Are Americans now stuck in animosity and anger that will undermine democracy, or can the nation pull out of it?

Politicians Divide

Our research finds that severe polarization is affected by three primary factors.

First, it is often stimulated by the rhetoric of political leaders who exploit the real grievances of voters. These politicians choose divisive issues to highlight in order to pursue their own political agenda.

In other words, what a leader says is as important as what she or he does.

Since launching his campaign, President Donald Trump has vilified so-called external enemies such as "criminal and rapist" Mexican immigrants, terrorist Muslims and foreign allies out to drain America's coffers through "unfair trade deficits." Now, the president is targeting internal enemies.

He has famously labeled the media "the enemy of the people" and recently accused the Democrats of unleashing an "angry mob" unfit to govern.

Such unprecedented attacks by a president of the United States seemed designed to discredit his critics and delegitimize his political opponents. But they also trigger the dynamics of polarized politics by reinforcing the notion that politics is an "us versus them" contest.

By August 2017, just eight months after Trump took office, three-quarters of Republicans had negative views of Democrats, and 70 percent of Democrats viewed Republicans negatively.

This was a large increase compared with the mid-1990s, when about 20 percent of each party had unfavorable views of the other party.

Even more disturbing for democracy, roughly half of voters of each party say the other party makes them feel afraid, and growing numbers view the policies of the other party as a threat to the nation.

America's recent political polarization did not begin with Trump. It has been growing since the 1990s and accelerated under

President Barack Obama, when the Tea Party formed in reaction to his election, and bipartisanship broke down in the Congress.

By 2016, 45 percent of Republicans felt threatened by Democratic policies, and 41 percent of Democrats viewed Republican policies as a threat, up nearly 10 points in just two years.

Our research shows that in extreme polarization, people feel distant from and suspicious of the "other" camp. At the same time, they feel loyal to, and trusting of, their own camp—without examining their biases or factual basis of their information.

Although this is a common phenomenon long identified by social psychology, it is even more pronounced in the age of social media 24-hour news cycles and more politicized media outlets who repeat and amplify the political attacks.

Most dangerously, words can unleash actual violence by avid supporters seeking approval from the leader or simply inspired to carry out an attack against the designated "enemy," as we saw when supporters of Hugo Chávez in Venezuela attacked a media mogul whom Chávez had labeled public enemy number one.

Similarly, last week an avid Trump supporter sent pipe bomb mailers to prominent Trump opponents, and the killings in a synagogue in Pittsburgh were carried out by a man who used similar language to Trump's assertion that the U.S. was being invaded by a caravan of Central Americans.

Polarization, though, is a two-way street.

Both Sides Now

How the political opposition reacts is the second factor explaining the impact of polarization on democracy.

If the opposition returns the bitter rhetoric with similar political hardball and demonizing language, they risk locking in place a cycle that leads to entrenching the politics of polarization.

A perceived political win may in fact prove to be an eventual defeat.

That happened in 2013 when the Democratic Party changed the long-standing rule that nominees to federal judgeships needed 60 Senate votes to end debate and move to a confirmation vote.

To overcome Republican obstruction under Obama, the Democrats who held a majority in the Senate at the time abandoned that rule and decreed that only 51 votes would be needed for all federal judgeships—except the Supreme Court.

Eventually the majority party becomes once again the minority. That's what happened when Republicans gained the majority in 2014 and blocked Obama's last nomination for a Supreme Court justice.

When Democrats retaliated by filibustering Trump's first nominee for the Supreme Court, the Republican Party escalated the fight and abolished the century-old filibuster rule even for the highest court in the land. They approved Justice Brett Kavanaugh with only a single Democratic vote.

Backing Away from Polarization

The third, and most difficult, obstacle is what our research found about the underlying basis of polarization.

When countries polarize around rifts that reflect unresolved debates present at the country's formation, then that polarization is most likely to be enduring and harmful.

The U.S. was founded on unequal citizenship rights for African-Americans, Native Americans and women. As these groups reasserted their rights in the 1960s civil rights movement and the 1970s women's movement, polarization around these rights and changing group status grew.

The same is true for the growing diversity of religion, gender and ethnicity in the workplace and society since the 1980s, which has become an added polarizing issue in U.S. politics.

Can the U.S. overcome the dynamics of polarization, where certain phenomena—divisive and demonizing rhetoric, tit-for-tat political retribution and long-standing unresolved rifts—lead to diminished democracy?

Our research shows that the most democratic of actions—participating in elections—is exactly the thing to do to help reduce polarization.

To avoid deepening the state of division and distrust that seems to pervade our society, both political leaders and citizens must play a part. Simply withdrawing from politics is not effective.

Citizens can protect themselves and their democracy by being aware of the political and psychological workings of polarization and the early warning signs of democratic erosion.

They can refuse to participate in the trap of demonizing politics, while insisting on voting massively against those who use polarizing methods.

Political leaders should be conscious that their words and actions can advance, prevent or reverse severe polarization.

For those who prioritize winning for their team above all, the realization that they will eventually be the losers of their re-engineered rules should be sobering—whether it is eliminating the filibuster in the U.S. Senate or the right to gerrymander electoral districts.

For those who have a broader perspective focused on the collective interests and welfare of the society, understanding the logic of polarization that blocks cooperative problem-solving could instill the courage to cross the divide rather than reciprocate pernicious polarizing strategies.

The ultimate solution to depolarize the contentiousness around national identity and citizenship rights that divides the U.S., however, requires addressing these debates head-on.

With a spirit of inquiry, generosity and openness, rather than blame and vilification, the U.S. can move past the bitter divisions that threaten the democratic foundations of the country.

> *"In his farewell address, George Washington warned the people of the perils of partisan disunity, but today America is at least in part defined by its Red State/Blue State divide."*

Political Parties in the US Have a Long and Often Confusing History

The Edge

In the following viewpoint, authors from The Edge discuss political parties in the United States throughout history. The authors examine how the parties have changed and shifted and the effect they have had on politics and elections. While the founders cautioned against partisan division, there is no question that is exactly where we've ended up. The authors attempt to explain how it happened, beginning with the first party system and ending with the sixth of today. The brief mention of third parties undercuts the effect they have had and could have. The Edge is a learning center that provides resources for teaching and guiding students.

As you read, consider the following questions:

1. Which parties were in America's first party system?
2. Which party did former slaves join, for the most part?
3. What caused the shift between the Republican and Democratic parties?

"Topics in US History: Political Parties," The Edge. Reprinted by permission.

The development over time of political parties is one of the most complicated yet significant topics in United States History. In his farewell address, George Washington warned the people of the perils of partisan disunity, but today America is at least in part defined by its Red State/Blue State divide. For students of history, knowing about the rise, fall, shifting, and flip-flopping of domestic political parties within the two-party system remains a pivotal skill in understanding the history of America.

1790s-1820s: The First Party System

For all intents and purposes, the first party system (and inter-party beef) in America compromised the Democratic Republicans, the party of Thomas Jefferson, and the Federalists, which was the party of George Washington's Secretary of Treasury, Alexander Hamilton. Hamilton and his crew called for a strong and unified federal government, with a nationalized banking system and diplomatic ties to Britain. Contrarily, Jefferson and his supporters desired ties to France and an emphasis on states' rights; they opposed pretty much any and all of the Federalists' agenda.

Into the early 19th century, after Jefferson's presidency, the Federalists lost popularity and petered out. The Democratic Republicans, the last men standing, emerged as the party to usher in "The Era of Good Feelings," thus ending the country's First Party System.

1820s-1850s: The Jacksonian Era and the Second Party System

By 1829, the traditional Democratic Republicans evolved into the Jacksonian Democrats, culminating in the presidency of Andrew Jackson, the divisive war hero, executive juggernaut, and Indian remover who would turn the party of Jefferson into the mighty modern Democrats. Though Jackson was loved by his supporters, his controversial policies—which many saw as abuses of power—influenced the establishment of the Whig Party in 1833. Essentially, this party existed to kick Jackson the Tyrant out of the White House, and so its problem was that it didn't really have any common platform or ideology at its core. As the debate over slavery got hot in the early 1850s, as well as because of its practical limitations and the deaths of its influential leaders, the party was disbanded.

1850s-1890s: The Third Party System

Post-Whig Party, the political era known as the Third Party System is associated with the emergence of the anti-slavery Republican Party in 1854, culminating in the party's candidate, Abraham Lincoln, winning the election of 1860. The Democrats, who were by now dominated by staunch pro-slavery representatives, weren't thrilled, and it was the Southern wing of this party that led the Succession movement, bringing about the Civil War. After the war, conflicts over Reconstruction dominated inter-party politics. Former slaves, for the most part, became Republicans, while in the South, bitterness over the war ensured that the Democrats would be the party of the defeated Confederate cause.

While in the North, as the century progressed, businessmen and skilled professionals grew attracted to the Republican platform because its emphasis on modernization and industry.

1890s-1930s: Fourth and Fifth Party Systems

This system maintained the two powers, Republicans and Democrats respectively, but it saw a major shift in each parties policies and central issues. Early on, it was the Republicans and their emphasis on big business that dominated the Progressive Era. But then, in 1929, the Stock Market crashed and everything got fudged up, culminating in President Franklin Roosevelt's ascendancy. FDR, a Northerner but a Democrat, formed the New Deal Coalition to create jobs and rebuild the economy. The one-sided results of the Election of 1932 demonstrated the shift in power from Republican to Democrat and symbolized FDR's clear political success.

Furthermore, Roosevelt's New Deal revolution and its promotion of civil rights programs led African Americans to change their party allegiances, which created a dramatic shift in constituencies. The Republicans, the party of Lincoln and abolition, could no longer count on the black vote.

1930s-Present: The Sixth (?) Party System and Beyond

Though some historians hold that the US remains immersed in the Fifth System, others argue that there have been major political schisms after WW2 that have helped contort and redefine the pretzel that is the modern political party framework, and thus the Fifth System has in fact made way for a Sixth. Evidence of this can be found in the results of Richard Nixon's Southern Strategy, the emergence of the Moral Majority in the late seventies, Ronald Reagan's success through coalition in the eighties, the Republican Revolution of 1994, anti-Bush sentiment, Obama's support as well as the backlash against him, and whatever's going on in the wild and wacky Election of 2016.

This article's been focusing on the major parties, and the minors haven't been discussed. Third parties have been influential in US History, both on the state and national level.

So there you have it, folks! Confused? Well, you should be. Though this article attempts to compile a discernible portrait, the true logic of America's political parties may in fact be illogical.

"After winning office, a party attempts to enact the priorities and positions of its base, which is not why the marginal voters supported it."

Maybe We're Not So Polarized After All

Clifton B. Parker

In the following viewpoint Clifton B. Parker interviews Morris Fiorina, a scholar who specializes in elections and public opinion. Fiorina's research indicates that the American public is not nearly as polarized in its political opinions as are politicians and pundits. In fact, says Fiorina, more Americans consider themselves moderates than as liberals or conservatives—a statistic that has not changed since 1976. Clifton B. Parker is a writer for the Stanford University News Service.

As you read, consider the following questions:

1. How does Morris Fiorina define polarization?
2. What is party sorting, and how does that contribute to the perception of polarization?
3. How does Fiorina say that the main parties fail their marginal voters in an attempt to satisfy the base? How does this affect policy and legislation?

"Politicians More Polarized than Voters, Stanford Political Scientist Finds," by Clifton B. Parker, Stanford University News Service, December 20, 2017. Reprinted by permission.

D espite widespread perceptions of rising political polarization in the United States, the American public is no more polarized than it was before the Reagan era, according to a Stanford scholar.

Morris Fiorina, a senior fellow at the Hoover Institution, studies elections and public opinion. He recently published the book, *Unstable Majorities: Polarization, Party Sorting and Political Stalemate*, which draws on his prior research and a variety of new data on the American electorate. He is also the Wendt Family Professor of Political Science.

The Stanford News Service recently interviewed Fiorina about the topic:

Are Voters More Polarized than Ever?

No. Although pundits and politicos make that claim every day, it's not true. If we take the electorate as a whole—without slicing it by partisanship, region or anything else—the public doesn't look any different than it did in 1976.

Polarization is the grouping of opinion around two extremes. No matter how we measure public opinion, this has not happened. In 2016, more Americans classified themselves as moderates than as liberals or conservatives; moreover, the numbers are virtually identical to those registered in 1976. The distribution of partisan identification flatly contradicts the polarization narrative: self-classified Republicans are no larger a proportion of the public than in the Eisenhower era, while self-identified Democrats are a significantly smaller proportion than in the 1960s. Forty percent of today's public declines to identify with either party.

Positions on specific issues support the same conclusion—the public favors a middle ground between the parties. On abortion, for example, the Democratic platform position is "any time, for any reason," while the Republican position is "never, no exceptions." The public says "sometimes, for some reasons."

What Is Causing Our Current Political Turbulence?

A process that is widely mistaken for polarization: what political scientists call "party sorting." The overall distribution of public opinion has not changed, but specific dimensions of it have become more highly correlated with partisanship. When I was in graduate school there were liberal Republican presidential candidates and U.S. senators and representatives. There were conservative Democratic presidential candidates and U.S. senators and representatives. Environmental protection was not a partisan issue in the early 1970s. Even in the 1980s, there were Democratic members of Congress who were pro-gun, and Republican members who were pro-choice. Today the issues align with partisanship and ideology—there has been a significant decline in cross-cutting cleavages, to use the older sociological terminology.

We can call this "partisan polarization" as long as we don't forget that there is still a big middle ground that is not part of it.

What Are the Consequences of "Party Sorting"?

A lot of the things that reasonable people complain about. A common complaint is that the two parties don't work together to solve our country's problems. It's difficult when the most liberal Republican in Congress is more conservative than the most conservative Democrat, as is the case today. And that's true across many issues. A generation ago, Republicans and Democrats who were opposed to each other on one issue might be allies on another issue. That's much less likely today. Another consequence is the geographic sorting of the parties. The Democratic base lies in the urban coastal states, while the Republican base lies in the Southern and Midwestern states.

In 1976 the Democrats nominated a "born again" Sunday school teacher (Jimmy Carter) from Georgia and the Republicans a country club moderate (Jerry Ford) from Michigan. Ford carried California and Connecticut. Carter carried Texas and Mississippi. It's hard to imagine that today.

What reinforces the difficulty of working together is the close party balance. Neither party enjoys majority support. Control of our national institutions flips back and forth. As University of Maryland political scientist Frances Lee documents, the congressional parties will reverse long-held policy positions rather than allow the other party to achieve legislative success. Winning control, not solving the country's problems, is the primary goal.

What Is the Role of Media, Polls, Swing Voters and Independents in the Rise of Populism or Other Political Movements?

In my book, I argue that the current electoral instability reflects the fact that we have two highly sorted parties, each of which tries to impose its narrow vision on a big, heterogeneous country. After winning office, a party attempts to enact the priorities and positions of its base, which is not why the marginal voters supported it. In the next election, some of the latter defect to the other party. Consider 2016 from the standpoint of a moderate, unattached voter. She has seen a Republican administration take the country into two interminable wars and preside over two economic crashes. Then she sees a Democratic administration fail to jail any of the miscreants responsible for the great crash, preside over a slow and uneven recovery and compile a less than stellar record in foreign affairs. Maybe, she wonders, these "experts" don't know as much as they think they do. Let's try something different. The fact that the so-called experts frequently tend to condescend to the broader public reinforces the allure of the outsider.

Are Political Parties Stronger or Weaker Today than Previously?

There's no single answer to that question. Clearly the ability of the legislative parties to enforce cohesion is much greater than a generation ago. On the other hand, the ability of the party to control nominations is probably lower than a generation ago. In

2016, Donald Trump rolled the Republican Party establishment and Bernie Sanders knocked the Democratic establishment on its heels. What is a party today? Parties are much more multifaceted than they used to be—not just party and government officials and a few big interest groups, but also donor networks, campaign consultants and pollsters, and issue activists.

Any Other Key Points You'd Like to Address?

Citizens should realize that nearly everyone featured in the political media is "abnormal" (in a statistical sense, but probably in other senses as well). The sorting process I have described is much more evident among the small minority that is most politically involved; most Americans are not, but these normal Americans are not the ones featured in the media. Bear in mind that less than 2 percent of the eligible electorate subscribes to the *New York Times*. About 1 percent of the electorate watches Fox News or Stanford's Rachel Maddow in the evening.

If you're one of those who watch Anderson Cooper on CNN (and I imagine that a lot of people reading this are), consider that about the same number of Americans at about the same time are watching Yogi Bear re-runs on Nick at Nite (admittedly, some of those viewers are too young to vote).

As always, most Americans are working, raising their families and otherwise going about their daily lives, not paying much attention to the political wars being fought by political elites.

Periodical and Internet Sources Bibliography

The following articles have been selected to supplement the diverse views presented in this chapter.

Thomas Carothers and Andrew O'Donohue, "How Americans Were Driven to Extremes: In the United States, Polarization Runs Particularly Deep," *Foreign Affairs*, 25 September 2019. https://www.foreignaffairs.com/articles/united-states/2019-09-25/how-americans-were-driven-extremes.

Michael Coblenz, "The Two-Party System Is Destroying America," *The Hill*, 28 January 2016. https://thehill.com/blogs/congress-blog/politics/267222-the-two-party-system-is-destroying-america.

Lee Drutman, "Why America's Two-Party System Is on a Collision Course with Our Constitutional Democracy," *Vox*, 26 March 2018. https://www.vox.com/polyarchy/2018/3/26/17163960/america-two-party-system-constitutional-democracy.

Glenn Geher, "The Polarization of America," *Psychology Today*, 14 August 2018. https://www.psychologytoday.com/us/blog/darwins-subterranean-world/201808/the-polarization-america.

Elaine Kamarck and Alexander R. Podkul, "What's Happening to the Democratic Party?" Brookings Institute, 14 September 2018. https://www.brookings.edu/blog/fixgov/2018/09/14/whats-happening-to-the-democratic-party/.

Martin Kelly, "The US Democratic Party: The Historic Roots of the Modern Democratic Party in the US," Thought.Co, 7 May 2019. https://www.thoughtco.com/democratic-party-104837.

Joseph Postell, "The Rise and Fall of Political Parties in America," The Heritage Foundation, 30 September 2018. https://www.heritage.org/political-process/report/the-rise-and-fall-political-parties-america.

Stephen M. Walt, "America's Polarization Is a Foreign Policy Problem, Too: The Fact That Democrats and Republicans Hate Each Other Is Making the United States Weaker," *Foreign Policy*, 11 March 2019. https://foreignpolicy.com/2019/03/11/americas-polarization-is-a-foreign-policy-problem-too/.

CHAPTER 2

Do Political Parties
Encourage Corruption?

Chapter Preface

The viewpoints in this chapter zero in on specifics of how parties influence elections and voters, not always in a positive way. This selection of perspectives addresses the question of the role parties play in political corruption.

The word *corruption* has several definitions. At one end, corruption is simply misuse of authority and power, by no means benign, but not always illegal. An official, whether elected or not, who has taken an oath to uphold the interests of the public could be considered corrupt when he or she puts private interests above the public interest. At the other extreme, corruption is a crime specified in the legal code, usually involving bribery or similar financial wrongdoing.

The viewpoints in the chapter explore ways political parties may or may not engage in corruption or encourage and enable corruption in elected officials. While some of the activities discussed in these viewpoints may not rise to the legal definition of corruption, some authors in this chapter argue that political parties and the structure of the US political system itself can support or enable corruption on the part of politicians.

The viewpoint authors explore questions and issues such as how Democratic Party rules for selecting a presidential nominee hurt Bernie Sanders and helped Hilary Clinton in the 2016 primary; the enormous influence of the National Rifle Association on the Republican Party; and how the influence of wealthy political donors takes the power of the vote away from ordinary citizens. The chapter closes with a reassuring viewpoint, arguing that, at least in some cases, politicians are responsive not just to party money and wealthy donors, but to ordinary citizens, as long as those citizens make their views known—and bother to vote.

> *"People are far more likely to participate in politics if they feel that government plays an important and beneficial role in their lives."*

Political Parties Sometimes Encourage Lack of Voter Participation

Sean McElwee

While the term corruption *often refers to crimes, such as bribery, in politics corruption sometimes takes forms that are not crimes* per se. *In the following viewpoint, Sean McElwee argues that the two major US parties are more accountable to the rich because wealthy people are more likely to give money to political candidates and, for a variety of structural reasons, are more likely to vote. The result, of course, is that parties are more responsive to the concerns of the wealthy than to the rest of the population. Sean McElwee is an activist and data scientist and cofounder of the nonprofit think tank Data for Progress.*

"Most Americans Don't Vote in Elections. Here's Why," by Sean McElwee, Al Jazeera America, July 27, 2015. Reprinted by permission.

As you read, consider the following questions:

1. What reasons does the author list for low voter turnout in the United States?
2. Why, according to the viewpoint, does the establishment of social programs, such as Social Security and the GI Bill, increase citizen participation?
3. Why does the author say that it is in the interest of the Republican Party to decrease the effectiveness of government?

New U.S. Census data released on July 19 confirm what we already knew about American elections: Voter turnout in the United States is among the lowest in the developed world. Only 42 percent of Americans voted in the 2014 midterm elections, the lowest level of voter turnout since 1978. And midterm voters tend to be older, whiter and richer than the general population. The aggregate number is important but turnout among different groups is even more crucial.

Politicians are more accountable and responsive to wealthy voters, not just because rich people vote in elections, but because they are also more likely to donate to campaigns or work on them to get their candidates elected. And the effects of the gap in voter turnout are far-reaching because, for many Americans, elections are one of the only ways in which they can participate in democracy.

Boosting Voter Participation

Gaps in voter turnout exacerbate the United States' already unequal political system. Its uniquely difficult electoral system is responsible for much of the low voter participation. This includes the practice of filling key offices during midterm or off-cycle elections, the odd Electoral College, a majoritarian rather than proportional system and the voter registration barrier, which leaves the responsibility for voter registration to citizens. (In most countries, the government conducts voter education and registration.) It doesn't help that

What Exactly Is Political Corruption?

Political corruption means the abuse of political power by the government leaders to extract and accumulate for private enrichment, and to use politically corrupt means to maintain their hold on power. However, abuse of political power for other purposes, such as repression of political opponents and general police brutality, is not considered political corruption. Political corruption takes place at the highest levels of the political system, and hence it can be differentiated from administrative or bureaucratic corruption. It can also be distinguished from business and private sector corruption.

Political corruption can be of two forms. The first one is which includes both accumulation and extraction and where government officials use and abuse their hold on power to extract from the private sector, from government revenues, and from the economy at large. Some of the examples of the above mentioned form of corruption are extraction, embezzlement, rent-seeking, plunder and even kleptocracy ("rule by thieves").

The second form of political corruption is one in which extracted resources (and public money) are used for power preservation and power extension purposes. This usually takes the form of favouritism and patronage politics. It includes a favouritist and politically motivated distribution of financial and material inducements, benefits, advantages, and spoils.

"Political Corruption Law and Legal Definition," AirSlate Legal Forms, Inc.

one of the two main political parties views reducing voter turnout as a key to its electoral success. Furthermore, the fact that the United States disenfranchises its many felons contributes to the low turnout.

To illustrate why the turnout gap matters, a recent study by political scientist Robert Erikson found that the median voter in 2008 in terms of income was at the 66th percentile for the general population. And as political scientist Michael Barber estimates, fewer than 3 percent of campaign donors, who give more than $200, make less than $50,000—almost the same as the median household income in the United States. Assuming that politicians respond to the median voter, they are less likely to favor policies of redistribution than they would if they responded to the median citizen.

There is also another, less recognized factor at play. In her 2005 book, "How Policies Make Citizens," political scientist Andrea Louise Campbell argued that government structures and policies could either facilitate or deter citizen participation in politics. For example, Campbell notes that the establishment of Social Security led to increased civic participation by the elderly (especially the poor), by motivating them to defend and seek the program's expansion. By contrast, the stigma associated with welfare programs such as Temporary Assistance to Needy Families (TANF) led to a decrease in voter turnout.

Other studies corroborate Campbell's findings. A 2010 study on the role of public policies in civic and political engagement found that initiatives such as Head Start, a federal program that provides early childhood education, health, nutrition and other services to low-income children and their families, increase political participation, while welfare and public housing assistance policies reduce it. Similarly, Suzanne Mettler, author of "Soldiers to Citizens," argues that the GI Bill, which provided many benefits to World War II veterans, boosted their civic participation. Veterans had a positive experience with the program and felt that they were treated with dignity and respect, which lead to greater political participation, not only through voting but also by boosting veterans' involvement in civic organizations.

As I've noted before, voters' affinity to and identification with political parties and their perception of the differences between the two parties also affect turnout. It's deleterious to voter participation to pretend that there are not substantive differences between Republicans and Democrats. Last year, the Progressive Change Institute, which promotes progressive policy response to political issues, asked 1,500 of the so-called "drop-off" voters, who voted for Barack Obama in 2012 but did not vote in the 2014 midterm election, what policies would motivate them to vote in 2016. Potential voters listed progressive policies such as debt-free college, universal pre-K and a living wage job guarantee.

Why Don't Americans Vote?

In a 2012 *USA Today* poll, 59 percent of non-voters said they were frustrated by the fact that "nothing ever gets done" in government while 54 percent cited "corruption" and 42 percent pointed to the lack of difference between the two parties. About 37 percent said politics doesn't make much difference in their lives.

These results suggest that the most effective Republican disenfranchisement strategy may not be voter ID laws, but grinding government to a halt. By forcing government shutdowns, Republican leaders and lawmakers have significantly reduced voter participation to historic lows. Less than 1 in 5 Americans believe that government works for the benefit of everyone. Furthermore, recent U.S. Supreme Court decisions such as *Buckley v. Valeo* and *Citizens United v. FEC*, which led to the influx of corporate cash into politics and the rise of the donor class, have together turned more people away from politics.

But we can't blame only conservatives for the low voter turnout. Many Americans forgo voting because they don't see differences between Democrats and Republicans. "Respondents who perceive a greater difference between the candidates ... are more likely to vote," political scientists Jan Leighley and Jonathan Nagler, write in their book, "Who Votes Now?" "Those in the top income quintile see a larger difference between the candidates on ideology than do those in the bottom quintile." Their findings support claims made in recent cross-national research and a previous study by political scientist David Brockington, in which he argues that when individuals feel ideological affinity to candidates, they are more likely to vote. In addition, "choice-rich environments," in which parties span a wider ideological range, also boost voter turnout.

Ahead of the 2016 elections, Democrats need to embrace popular progressive policies to convince potential voters that they are indeed different and that they offer real solutions. Americans must also fight back against voter suppression attempts, among other things, by demanding automatic voter registration. Moreover, in order to reduce the power of money in politics and limit the influence of the donor class, lawmakers must work to increase the power of the people through public financing and strict lobbying regulations.

But these steps aren't enough. Voters must also pressure the candidates to put forward a vision that benefits the middle and lower class. People are far more likely to participate in politics if they feel that government plays an important and beneficial role in their lives. Policies such as debt-free college, universal child-care and pre-K education, a higher minimum wage and living wage job guarantees could increase voter turnout and civic engagement. American democracy is not for sale. The voting booth is a potent force against the power of plutocracy.

> *"Superdelegates are drawn from entrenched party leadership, and in 2016, at least 63 of the 712 total were registered lobbyists, and 32 more 'shadow lobbyists,' some of which were associated with big banks, payday lenders and large corporations."*

The 2016 Democratic Primary Was Rigged

Heather Gautney

The previous viewpoint focused mostly on corruption in the Republican Party. In the following viewpoint, Heather Gautney targets the Democrats. The author explains how the rules of the Democratic primary disenfranchise many voters. She argues that this is what kept Bernie Sanders from being elected as the 2016 Democratic nominee. Heather Gautney is associate professor of sociology at Fordham University, author of Crashing the Party: From the Bernie Sanders Campaign to a Progressive Movement, *and a member of Sanders's 2016 presidential campaign.*

As you read, consider the following questions:

1. What are superdelegates, and why are they unfair, according to the author?
2. What reforms does the author suggest? What reforms have been suggested by the party?
3. Does the system of superdelegates seem democratic to you? Why or why not?

Ask countless Bernie Sanders supporters, and they'll tell you a big reason he lost the Democratic party primaries is simple: the process was rigged. In one state after another, the votes by party elites—so-called "superdelegates"—counted more than those of regular members. And arduous voting requirements meant that countless people who would have voted for Sanders were denied that right. If the Democrats want any hope of voting Trump out of the White House, it is urgent they fix this broken system before the next election.

As a member of Sanders' campaign, I'll never forget watching the primary votes being counted for Michigan, one of the key states that decided the 2016 election. Sanders' "pledged delegate count"—which reflected the number of votes he received from rank-and-file Democrats—exceeded Clinton's by four. But after the superdelegates cast their ballots, the roll call registered "Clinton 76, Sanders 67".

This repeated itself in other states. In Indiana, Sanders won the vote 44 to 39, but, after the superdelegates had their say, Clinton was granted 46 delegates, versus Sanders' 44. In New Hampshire, where Sanders won the vote by a gaping margin (60% to 38%) and set a record for the largest number of votes ever, the screen read "16 Sanders, 16 Clinton".

Sanders "lost" those states because hundreds of superdelegates had pledged their votes long before the primaries and caucuses began. By including those prearranged votes, running media tallies reinforced the inevitability of a Clinton win and the common perception that the Democratic primary was "rigged". In June, the Associated Press went so far as to call the primary in Clinton's favor—before Californians even had a chance to cast their votes.

During the New York primary, between 3 and 4 million "unaffiliated" voters were disenfranchised due to a statute that required changing one's party affiliation 25 days prior to the previous general election. In 2016, that deadline was 193 days before election day. Over a third of under-30 voters—Sanders' core constituency—weren't registered to any political party. When those young people tried to vote, they were turned away.

In New York and other Democratic-leaning states, primaries have serious consequences. For this year's New York state primary, the deadline for unaffiliated voters to register Democratic is 11 months before the actual vote, a requirement that tilts the playing field in favor of incumbents. Unaffiliated voters wishing to support Cynthia Nixon's bid for governor, for example, will never have had a chance to vote for her, because that deadline passed before she announced her candidacy. The Democratic party, in turn, forfeited its chance to attract millions of independent and unaffiliated voters to participate in its primary.

In 2016, the progressive grassroots wing of the Democratic party, which strongly supported Sanders, raised persistent alarms about the blatant structural bias of the primary system. The result was the formation of a tripartite Unity Reform Commission (with 10 representatives from the Clinton campaign, eight for Sanders, and three appointed by the chair).

The outcome of the election—Trump's victory, widely perceived as a populist rejection of establishment politics—only increased the significance of the commission's work, for soul-searching Democrats stung by bitter defeat. The commission's consensus-drawn report, issued last December and endorsed by the Democratic party national chairman, Tom Perez, recommends that the number of superdelegates be reduced by 60%, and that state parties enact same-day voter registration and same-day party-switching. As an enforcement mechanism, state parties that don't comply can be docked party convention delegates.

This summer, the Democratic National Committee (DNC) will consider these and other recommendations. These deliberations could fundamentally reshape the Democratic party, and American politics, for many years to come.

A "yes" vote for the Commission's recommendations would diffuse the power of the Democratic party establishment and open the party to more progressive ideas and candidates. In places like New York, this could empower the progressive wing of the party, combat party-sanctioned voter suppression, and bring much-needed new blood to local and state politics.

Such a move could also recover some of the Democrats' lost base. During Obama's time as president, the Democratic party lost both chambers of Congress, nearly a thousand seats in state legislatures, and half of state governorships. In many parts of the country, Democrats have almost no political influence at all. The blue wave expected in 2018 could easily lose force if Democrats remain locked in internal struggles for control, rather than work together to expand their political horizon.

In the wake of misconduct by past party officials, such reforms could also help restore lost credibility by preventing those in power from putting their thumbs on the scale and allowing establishment politicians and big money undue influence. Superdelegates are drawn from entrenched party leadership, and in 2016, at least 63 of the 712 total were registered lobbyists, and 32 more "shadow lobbyists", some of which were associated with big banks, payday lenders and large corporations.

More profoundly, however, the reforms could help salve Americans' justified skepticism regarding our "rigged" political system—and finally live up to the promise of one-person, one-vote. A no vote, on the other hand, would have the opposite effect: severely undermine the Democratic party's legitimacy as a democratic party, and risk repeating the grave mistakes that got us where we are now.

> *"One thing is clear: Sanders isn't enthusiastic about being part of the Democratic club, or any club for that matter."*

Bernie Sanders Isn't Much of a Democrat, but He Doesn't Have to Be

Linda Qiu

In the previous viewpoint the author argued that the Democratic Party had rigged the 2016 presidential nomination against Bernie Sanders. In the following viewpoint, Linda Qiu argues that Sanders is not even a Democrat—or at least has not consistently represented himself as one throughout his political career. Yet, historically, being affiliated with the party is not a requirement for running for office under its banner. Qui explains the complex relationship between Sanders and the Democratic Party to shed, perhaps, some light on the vexed relationship between them. Linda Qiu is a fact-checker and political reporter for the New York Times. *At the time of this writing, she worked for the fact-checking service PolitiFact.*

As you read, consider the following questions:

1. According to the viewpoint, Bernie Sanders has been somewhat inconsistent in his party affiliations. Does running as a Democrat commit him to being a Democrat?
2. Does ambivalence on the part of both Sanders and the Democratic Party affect the argument made in the previous viewpoint?
3. Why, according to the author, did Sanders lobby to join the Democratic caucus in the US Senate?

Bernie Sanders is called many things: independent, progressive, socialist, democratic socialist, social democrat, communist, Intrepid, the Vermont Bonecrusher, etc.

But what about just plain, old "Democrat"?

"Bernie is a Democrat 'some days,'" California Sen. Barbara Boxer, who supports Hillary Clinton, tweeted glibly on Feb. 3.

Responding to Boxer's criticism during that night's town hall in New Hampshire, Sanders said, "Of course I am a Democrat and running for the Democratic nomination."

Despite this certainty, Sanders seems uncommitted to being committed to the party. His Senate website and press materials continue to label him as an "independent" while his campaign website lists him as a "Democratic candidate." In his home state of Vermont, there is no party registration.

So can Sanders accurately claim to be unaffiliated with a political party while still running for the Democratic nomination and sometimes calling himself a Democrat?

It may seem oxymoronic, but yes, he can.

The 40-Year Outsider

Sanders' electoral history places him firmly in the independent camp, but also shows that he has been gradually moving away from the far left.

Between 1972 and 1976, Sanders was the nominee of the anti-capitalist, anti-war Liberty Union Party of Vermont in two Senate and two gubernatorial elections in Vermont. He lost all four races and resigned from the party in 1977, calling it "sad and tragic," according to Greg Guma, author of *The People's Republic: Vermont and the Sanders Revolution.*

In 1981, Sanders made an independent bid for mayor of Burlington as a self-described socialist. He won by 10 votes over the city's Democratic mayor and two other independents, and went on to win three more terms.

Democrats and leftists disagree on where Sanders' political allegiances were during this decade.

Liberty Union Party co-founder Peter Diamondstone doesn't buy Sanders' claims to independence. He told the Daily Caller that Sanders "became a full-time Democrat" in 1984, when he campaigned for Democratic presidential candidate Walter Mondale.

Yet Sanders continued to fight with the party locally and his "goal was the destroy Democrats," Maurice Mahoney, the head of Burlington's Democratic Party in the 1980s, told Politico. He also mounted independent challenges against Democrats, including Vermont's first female Democratic governor in 1984, and reiterated that he had no party affiliation.

"I am not now, nor have I ever been, a liberal Democrat," he said in a 1985 *New England Monthly* profile, according to *Politico.*

"Socialist is the political and economic philosophy I hold, not a party I run under," he explained in 1988, when he unsuccessfully ran for Congress.

Partly in the Club

Running for Congress as an independent in 1989, Sanders penned an op-ed in the *New York Times* calling the two parties "tweedle-dee" and "tweedle-dum." After he won a seat in the House of Representatives, he continued to hold the Democratic Party at a rhetorical arm's length even as he moved closer to them.

After calling it "ideologically bankrupt," Sanders lobbied for admission into the Democratic caucus for practical reasons (getting coveted committee assignments, mustering votes for bills), according to news reports from his first year in Congress. But party leaders wouldn't let him join as he refused to become a Democrat.

So in 1991, Sanders along with four liberal Democrats founded the Congressional Progressive Caucus and he became its chairman. During his second year in office, Sanders continued to agitate and criticize Democrats, lumping them in with Republicans and calling both parties' tax proposals "grossly inadequate."

At some point, Sanders began to win the goodwill of Democratic leadership, all the while refusing to join the party.

A month before he was re-elected to a third term in 1994, House Democrats blessed his claim for a leadership role on one of his committees. Sanders had no Democratic challenger that year, and a spokesperson for his Republican opponent called Sanders "an adjunct to the Democratic Party" according to the *Washington Post*.

The party backed Sanders' 1996 re-election bid over one of their own. Burlington lawyer and Democrat Jack Long, after being informed that the party was committed to Sanders, told the *Washington Post* that he felt like he was "caught in a Kafka play." Sanders wouldn't have another Democratic opponent until 2004.

By 1997, Sanders was still not a member of the House Democratic Caucus nor a Democrat. But he voted with the party more often than the average Democrat (95 percent of the time opposed to 80 percent). Keeping good to their promise, Democratic leadership gave Sanders a subcommittee chairmanship over a freshman Democrat.

When he ran for the Senate a decade later in 2006, still as an independent, the party worked to stop Democratic candidates from running against him, and he was endorsed by numerous state and national Democrats.

You Are What You Say You Are

In his 2016 presidential bid, Sanders seems to oscillate between labeling himself as a Democrat and being an independent. But that's neither inaccurate nor particularly unusual, experts said.

Unlike elsewhere in the world, joining the two major parties isn't contingent upon membership fees or an application process. Party leaders also don't have the power to say someone isn't a Democrat or a Republican.

So political affiliation in the United States is a matter of self-identification, in both the governing system and the party organizations, experts said. That allows Sanders and other elected officials to be flexible.

For example, Pennsylvania Sen. Arlen Specter switched from Republican to Democrat in office in 2009, while Connecticut Sen. Joe Lieberman became an "Independent Democrat" after losing the Democratic primary, pointed out Daniel Holt, an assistant historian in the Senate Historical Office.

"There is nothing official to mark their party membership," Holt said.

"So it certainly does happen that candidates switch into and out of independent status, and I suppose they're called by whatever party they're running as at the time," said Marjorie Hershey, a professor of political science at Indiana University who specializes in political parties.

Sanders listed the Democratic Party as his party affiliation in his statement of candidacy. At the start of his campaign, he still seemed uncomfortable self-identifying as a Democrat.

When asked if he would officially join the party on April 30, 2015, when he announced his candidacy, Sanders said, "No, I am an independent who is going to be working with the —" cutting himself off mid-sentence.

In November, Sanders announced that he was full-fledged Democrat and declared as a Democrat in New Hampshire. But, as we previously noted, he's still calling himself an independent in some cases, so it's unclear how committed Sanders is to any label. The Sanders campaign did not get back to us.

Experts said it probably doesn't matter to his candidacy.

"The freedom of association part of the First Amendment protects political parties. If they want to nominate a non-member, they can do that," said Richard Winger, an expert on ballot access.

Winger pointed out several instances of a party nominating a non-member: 1872 when the Democratic Party chose Republican Horace Greeley; in 1864 when the Republican Party chose Democrat Andrew Johnson; and in 1952 when the Republican Party picked independent Dwight Eisenhower (who promptly changed his party registration).

Robert Wigton, a political science professor at Eckerd College who wrote *The Parties in Court,* said he'd call Sanders an independent for now, given how little the senator has said on the topic. But as he gets closer to the nomination, he'll make the switch and "probably try to shed that 'socialist label' if he gets close to a general election ballot."

One thing is clear: Sanders isn't enthusiastic about being part of the Democratic club, or any club for that matter.

"He was never really a party guy," Guma, the author of the book on Sanders' legacy in Vermont, told the *Daily Beast.* "His career was to be a voice and a candidate."

> "Frustrated by the lack of leadership in Washington, some Americans began to develop their own solutions, including the establishment of new political parties and organizations to directly address the problems they faced."

Political Corruption in the Post–Civil War Era Led to Dramatic Political Realignments

P. Scott Corbett, Volker Janssen, John M. Lund, Todd Pfannestiel, Paul Vickery, and Sylvie Waskiewicz

Previous viewpoints have examined instances of modern-day corruption. In the following viewpoint P. Scott Corbett, Volker Janssen, John M. Lund, Todd Pfannestiel, Paul Vickery, and Sylvie Waskiewicz consider the history of political corruption in the United States since the end of the Civil War and how that eventually led to the establishment of new political parties and alliances. P. Scott Corbett, Volker Janssen, John M. Lund, Todd Pfannestiel, and Paul Vickery are historians and authors of the OpenStax textbook US History. *Sylvie Waskiewicz is an editor of academic publications and textbooks.*

As you read, consider the following questions:

1. What challenges did the nation face in the immediate aftermath of the Civil War, according to the viewpoint?
2. Why did presidents have so little power in the Gilded Age? How is that similar to current times?
3. What was "The Great Betrayal" and how did that affect US political alignments?

The challenges Americans faced in the post–Civil War era extended far beyond the issue of Reconstruction and the challenge of an economy without slavery. Political and social repair of the nation was paramount, as was the correlative question of race relations in the wake of slavery. In addition, farmers faced the task of cultivating arid western soils and selling crops in an increasingly global commodities market, while workers in urban industries suffered long hours and hazardous conditions at stagnant wages.

Farmers, who still composed the largest percentage of the U.S. population, faced mounting debts as agricultural prices spiraled downward. These lower prices were due in large part to the cultivation of more acreage using more productive farming tools and machinery, global market competition, as well as price manipulation by commodity traders, exorbitant railroad freight rates, and costly loans upon which farmers depended. For many, their hard work resulted merely in a continuing decline in prices and even greater debt. These farmers, and others who sought leaders to heal the wounds left from the Civil War, organized in different states, and eventually into a national third-party challenge, only to find that, with the end of Reconstruction, federal political power was stuck in a permanent partisan stalemate, and corruption was widespread at both the state and federal levels.

As the Gilded Age unfolded, presidents had very little power, due in large part to highly contested elections in which relative popular majorities were razor-thin. Two presidents won the Electoral College without a popular majority. Further undermining their efficacy was a Congress comprising mostly politicians operating on the principle of political patronage. Eventually, frustrated by the lack of leadership in Washington, some Americans began to develop their own solutions, including the establishment of new political parties and organizations to directly address the problems they faced. Out of the frustration wrought by war and presidential political impotence, as well as an overwhelming pace of industrial change, farmers and workers formed a new grassroots reform movement that, at the end of the century, was eclipsed by an even larger, mostly middle-class, Progressive movement. These reform efforts did bring about change—but not without a fight.

The Gilded Age

Mark Twain coined the phrase "Gilded Age" in a book he co-authored with Charles Dudley Warner in 1873, *The Gilded Age: A Tale of Today*. The book satirized the corruption of post–Civil War society and politics. Indeed, popular excitement over national growth and industrialization only thinly glossed over the stark economic inequalities and various degrees of corruption of the era. Politicians of the time largely catered to business interests in exchange for political support and wealth. Many participated in graft and bribery, often justifying their actions with the excuse that corruption was too widespread for a successful politician to resist. The machine politics of the cities, specifically Tammany Hall in New York, illustrate the kind of corrupt, but effective, local and national politics that dominated the era.

Nationally, between 1872 and 1896, the lack of clear popular mandates made presidents reluctant to venture beyond the interests of their traditional supporters. As a result, for nearly a quarter of a century, presidents had a weak hold on power, and legislators were reluctant to tie their political agendas to such weak leaders. On the contrary, weakened presidents were more susceptible to support various legislators' and lobbyists' agendas, as they owed tremendous favors to their political parties, as well as to key financial contributors, who helped them garner just enough votes to squeak into office through the Electoral College. As a result of this relationship, the rare pieces of legislation passed were largely responses to the desires of businessmen and industrialists whose support helped build politicians' careers.

What was the result of this political malaise? Not surprisingly, almost nothing was accomplished on the federal level. However, problems associated with the tremendous economic growth during this time continued to mount. More Americans were moving to urban centers, which were unable to accommodate the massive numbers of working poor. Tenement houses with inadequate sanitation led to widespread illness. In rural parts of the country, people fared no better. Farmers were unable to cope with the challenges of low prices for their crops and exorbitant costs for everyday goods. All around the country, Americans in need of solutions turned further away from the federal government for help, leading to the rise of fractured and corrupt political groups.

Mark Twain and the Gilded Age

Mark Twain wrote *The Gilded Age: A Tale of Today* with his neighbor, Charles Dudley Warner, as a satire about the corrupt politics and lust for power that he felt characterized American society at the time. The book, the only novel Twain ever co-authored, tells of the characters' desire to sell their land to the federal government and become rich. It takes aim at both the government in Washington and those Americans, in the South and elsewhere, whose lust for money and status among the newly rich in the nation's capital leads them to corrupt and foolish choices.

In the following conversation from Chapter Fifty-One of the book, Colonel Sellers instructs young Washington Hawkins on the routine practices of Congress:

> "Now let's figure up a little on, the preliminaries. I think Congress always tries to do as near right as it can, according to its lights. A man can't ask any fairer than that. The first preliminary it always starts out on, is to clean itself, so to speak. It will arraign two or three dozen of its members, or maybe four or five dozen,

for taking bribes to vote for this and that and the other bill last winter."

"It goes up into the dozens, does it?"

"Well, yes; in a free country likes ours, where any man can run for Congress and anybody can vote for him, you can't expect immortal purity all the time—it ain't in nature. Sixty or eighty or a hundred and fifty people are bound to get in who are not angels in disguise, as young Hicks the correspondent says; but still it is a very good average; very good indeed. . . . Well, after they have finished the bribery cases, they will take up cases of members who have bought their seats with money. That will take another four weeks."

"Very good; go on. You have accounted for two-thirds of the session."

"Next they will try each other for various smaller irregularities, like the sale of appointments to West Point cadetships, and that sort of thing— . . . "

"How long does it take to disinfect itself of these minor impurities?"

"Well, about two weeks, generally."

"So Congress always lies helpless in quarantine ten weeks of a session. That's encouraging."

The book was a success, in part because it amused people even as it excoriated the politics of the day. For this humor, as well as its astute analysis, Twain and Warner's book still offers entertainment and insight today.

The Election of 1876 Sets the Tone

In many ways, the presidential election of 1876 foreshadowed the politics of the era, in that it resulted in one of the most controversial results in all of presidential history. The country was in the middle of the economic downturn caused by the Panic of 1873, a downturn that would ultimately last until 1879, all but assuring that Republican incumbent Ulysses S. Grant would not be reelected. Instead, the Republican Party nominated a three-time governor from Ohio, Rutherford B. Hayes. Hayes was a popular candidate who advocated for both "hard money"—an economy based upon gold currency transactions—to protect against inflationary pressures and civil service reform, that is, recruitment based upon merit and qualifications, which was to replace the practice of handing out government jobs as "spoils." Most importantly, he had no significant political scandals in his past, unlike his predecessor Grant, who suffered through the Crédit Mobilier of America scandal. In this most notorious example of Gilded Age corruption, several congressmen accepted cash and stock bribes in return for appropriating inflated federal funds for the construction of the transcontinental railroad.

The Democrats likewise sought a candidate who could champion reform against growing political corruption. They found their man in Samuel J. Tilden, governor of New York and a self-made millionaire, who had made a successful political career fighting corruption in New York City, including spearheading the prosecution against Tammany Hall Boss William Tweed, who was later jailed. Both parties tapped into the popular mood of the day, each claiming to champion reform and promising an end to the corruption that had become rampant in Washington. Likewise, both parties promised an end to post–Civil War Reconstruction.

The campaign was a typical one for the era: Democrats shone a spotlight on earlier Republican scandals, such as the Crédit Mobilier affair, and Republicans relied upon the bloody shirt campaign, reminding the nation of the terrible human toll of the war against southern confederates who now reappeared in national politics under the mantle of the Democratic Party. President Grant previously had great success with the "bloody shirt" strategy in the 1868 election, when Republican supporters attacked Democratic candidate Horatio Seymour for his sympathy with New York City draft rioters during the war. In 1876, true to the campaign style of the day, neither Tilden nor Hayes actively campaigned for office, instead relying upon supporters and other groups to promote their causes.

Fearing a significant African American and white Republican voter turnout in the South, particularly in the wake of the Civil Rights Act of 1875, which further empowered African Americans with protection in terms of public accommodations, Democrats relied upon white supremacist terror organizations to intimidate blacks and Republicans, including physically assaulting many while they attempted to vote. The Redshirts, based in Mississippi and the Carolinas, and the White League in Louisiana, relied upon intimidation tactics similar to the Ku Klux Klan but operated in a more open and organized fashion with the sole goal of restoring Democrats to political predominance in the South. In several instances, Redshirts would attack freedmen who attempted to vote, whipping them openly in the streets while simultaneously hosting barbecues to attract Democratic voters to the polls. Women throughout South Carolina began to sew red flannel shirts for the men to wear as a sign of their political views; women themselves began wearing red ribbons in their hair and bows about their waists.

The result of the presidential election, ultimately, was close. Tilden won the popular vote by nearly 300,000 votes; however, he had only 184 electoral votes, with 185 needed to proclaim formal victory. Three states, Florida, Louisiana, and South Carolina, were in dispute due to widespread charges of voter fraud and miscounting. Questions regarding the validity of one of the three electors in Oregon cast further doubt on the final vote; however, that state subsequently presented evidence to Congress confirming all three electoral votes for Hayes.

As a result of the disputed election, the House of Representatives established a special electoral commission to determine which candidate won the challenged electoral votes of these three states. In what later became known as the Compromise of 1877, Republican Party leaders offered southern Democrats an enticing deal. The offer was that if the commission found in favor of a Hayes victory, Hayes would order the withdrawal of the remaining U.S. troops from those three southern states, thus allowing the collapse of the radical Reconstruction governments of the immediate post–Civil

War era. This move would permit southern Democrats to end federal intervention and control their own states' fates in the wake of the end of slavery.

After weeks of deliberation, the electoral commission voted eight to seven along straight party lines, declaring Hayes the victor in each of the three disputed states. As a result, Hayes defeated Tilden in the electoral vote by a count of 185–184 and became the next president. By April of that year, radical Reconstruction ended as promised, with the removal of federal troops from the final two Reconstruction states, South Carolina and Louisiana. Within a year, Redeemers—largely Southern Democrats—had regained control of the political and social fabric of the South.

Although unpopular among the voting electorate, especially among African Americans who referred to it as "The Great Betrayal," the compromise exposed the willingness of the two major political parties to avoid a "stand-off" via a southern Democrat filibuster, which would have greatly prolonged the final decision regarding the election. Democrats were largely satisfied to end Reconstruction and maintain "home rule" in the South in exchange for control over the White House. Likewise, most realized that Hayes would likely be a one-term president at best and prove to be as ineffectual as his pre–Civil War predecessors.

Perhaps most surprising was the lack of even greater public outrage over such a transparent compromise, indicative of the little that Americans expected of their national government. In an era where voter turnout remained relatively high, the two major political parties remained largely indistinguishable in their agendas as well as their propensity for questionable tactics and backroom deals. Likewise, a growing belief in laissez-faire principles as opposed to reforms and government intervention (which many Americans believed contributed to the outbreak of the Civil War) led even more Americans to accept the nature of an inactive federal government.

> "Over the past 40 years, many of the post-Watergate campaign finance reforms have been eliminated or severely eroded, craftily and relentlessly by the powers that be, including both major political parties."

Rollbacks of Post-Watergate Reforms Have Eroded US Democracy

Charles Lewis

Money fuels politics, but as we've seen in previous viewpoints, it can also fuel corruption. In the following viewpoint, Charles Lewis examines the effects of a four-decades-long trend of weakening legislation to prevent corruption in politics. This viewpoint looks particularly at Citizens United, a Supreme Court case that allowed unlimited campaign donations by corporations. Charles Lewis is a journalist and professor at American University.

"Dark Money: Five Years after Citizens United," by Charles Lewis, The Conversation, January 30, 2015. https://theconversation.com/dark-money-five-years-after-citizens-united-36872.

As you read, consider the following questions:

1. According to this viewpoint, two billionaire brothers spent as much on the 2016 election as all political parties combined. What are the implications of this, based on what you've learned so far about political parties?
2 Why did Nixon's resignation prompt reform in campaign laws?
3. Why have those laws been weakened in the years since?

This week's news brings an important "ah hah" moment.

The conservative billionaire brothers Charles and David Koch of Koch Industries and their political network of donors and opaque outside groups are planning to spend a stratospheric $889 million in the 2016 presidential and congressional elections.

That is more than double what they and their network spent in 2012, an amount so stupendous that it will be "on par with the spending by (political) parties"

What a way to mark the fifth anniversary of the Supreme Court's Citizens United decision that paved the way for unlimited political spending by outside groups.

It Wasn't Always So

There was a time and a place, far, far away, when Americans found such outsized political influence not only unseemly, it was actually illegal.

Consider the US$2.1 million that insurance mogul W Clement Stone gave to incumbent President Richard Nixon's 1972 reelection campaign and to the Republican Party, then a record. That sum would be equal in today's inflation-adjusted dollars to $11.9 million, underwhelming now compared to the unseemly sums of cash swirling around these days.

What a long, strange trip it's been, to paraphrase the Grateful Dead.

In the wake of Watergate, the worst political scandal in American history in which Richard Nixon's White House, his political party and numerous corporations secretly but rambunctiously broke federal laws, more than 70 people, including White House aides and Cabinet officials, were convicted of crimes related to the Watergate break-in and its cover up.

In the wake of Nixon's unprecedented resignation, in August 1974, the new Republican President Gerald Ford signed important reform legislation into law.

The new laws established stricter campaign contribution limits and public disclosure requirements, a federal presidential campaign matching fund system and a new regulatory agency, the Federal Election Commission.

As President Gerald R. Ford said, "The times demand this legislation."

Three months later, the Republicans were utterly humiliated in the 1974 elections. The same happened again in 1976. It was the party's electoral nadir of the past half century.

Indeed, former GOP chairman and Senator Bill Brock told me years later the public's repugnance towards them was so bad that worried Republican elders had seriously considered changing the party's name.

But that was then.

Rolling Back the Reforms

Over the past 40 years, many of the post-Watergate campaign finance reforms have been eliminated or severely eroded, craftily and relentlessly by the powers that be, including both major political parties.

Unfortunately, now even the bedrock value of transparency itself is under siege, criticized for impairing the ability to compromise and weakening government.

And as for the once-humiliated Republicans, they have certainly made their comeback. They control both Houses of Congress, their appointees lead the US Supreme Court and, with the 2016 presidential election looming, they are girding their loins to win the trifecta of all three major branches of government.

How did all of this happen?

It's a long story, but essentially, the US Supreme Court in a series of rulings that began in 1976 and continues to today, removed many of the post-Watergate campaign contribution limits and other reforms.

Citizens United v. the Federal Election Commission

The most significant Court decision of all was the one that occurred on January 21, 2010, in which the Court ruled that the First Amendment forbids the government from limiting independent political expenditures by a nonprofit corporation.

These principles have also now been extended to for-profit corporations, labor unions and other organizations. In other words, pretty much anything goes. Or, as one exasperated observer put it, "the United States Supreme Court struck down barriers to corporate control of democracy with its 2010 *Citizens United v. Federal Election Commission* ruling."

Five years ago and over 35 years after Nixon's resignation, Justice John Paul Stevens denounced the controversial Citizens United decision in his dissent

> "The rule announced today—that Congress must treat corporations exactly like human speakers in the political realm— represents a radical change in the law. The court's decision is at war with the views of generations of Americans…"

Justice Anthony Kennedy, voting with the majority, attempted to reassure skeptics, arguing that transparency and disclosure would let citizens "see whether elected officials are 'in the pocket' of so-called moneyed interests."

But since then, of course, untraceable donations are on the rise. We now have literally hundreds of millions of secret dollars washing into the US political process.

As Justice Stevens put it so well,

"Corruption can take many forms. Bribery may be the paradigm case. But the difference between selling a vote and selling access is a matter of degree, not kind. And selling access is not qualitatively different from giving special preference to those who spent money on one's behalf. Corruption operates along a spectrum, and the majority's apparent belief that quid pro quo arrangements can be neatly demarcated from other improper influences does not accord with the theory or reality of politics."

Five months after writing that, Stevens, a Republican who had been appointed to the Court in 1975 by President Ford, retired from the bench at the age of 90.

The amount of completely or partially undisclosed money, often described as "dark money" spent by outside organizations in the 2014 elections is estimated to have been over $200 million, according to public records analyzed by the respected Center for Responsive Politics in Washington.

A record $6.3 billion was spent on the 2012 presidential and congressional elections and the "growing shadow of political money" will become even larger—the 2016 elections may be the first $8 billion presidential and congressional election cycle. For years, the United States has already had the longest and most expensive presidential elections on Planet Earth.

The Citizens United decision has significantly exacerbated our precarious, undemocratic condition.

> *"Research suggests that members of Congress respond to more than just the power of money. That research found that members of Congress respond more to voters in their districts than to nonvoters when making policy."*

Members of Congress Respond to More Than Money—Sometimes

Jan Leighley and Jennifer Oser

Much of the material in this chapter has focused on the corrupting influence of money in politics. In this closing viewpoint Jan Leighley and Jennifer Oser take a look at a more cheerful aspect of our democracy. The authors argue that citizens—even those without the power money can buy—can at least occasionally have an influence on their elected leaders. But it takes hard work—and showing up to vote. Jan Leighley is Professor of Government at American University School of Public Affairs. Jennifer Oser is Senior Lecturer of Politics and Government at Ben-Gurion University of the Negev.

As you read, consider the following questions:

1. What are ways, beyond protest movements, that ordinary citizens can effectively make their wishes known to their elected officials?
2. Other than wealthy donors, who is more likely to get the attention of members of Congress, according to the authors? Why?
3. Why might local activism be more effective than national activism?

D oes citizen activism really affect the actions of elected officials? Despite the ubiquitous role of money in campaigns, elections and policymaking, some citizens clearly still believe in the power of protest.

In the month of December 2017 alone, an organization called The Crowd Counting Consortium "tallied 796 protests, demonstrations, strikes, marches, sit-ins and rallies," some of them featuring thousands of people, across the country. Over the past year, the offices of many members of Congress and other elected officials have been jammed with constituents voicing their opinions on the Affordable Care Act, the immigration program called DACA, abortion and sexual harassment, among others.

But does all of this sign waving and sitting in actually influence elected officials?

As social scientists, we have long been interested in political participation and online activism. We used this knowledge to design a study that looks at whether activism changes the votes of elected officials—and whether the effect is strong enough to mitigate the power of donated money.

What we found is that citizens can make their voices heard—at least some of the time.

Activism, an American Tradition

Signing petitions, contacting officials and protesting are potentially powerful because congressional elections occur only every other year, while representatives cast votes on important issues much more frequently.

The country's founders believed deeply in the right of citizens to act on their political beliefs. They enshrined that right in the First Amendment.

Protests—from the original Tea Party in 1773 to the 1960s civil rights marches to abortion clinic activists in recent years—offer dramatic examples of citizens making their voices heard. But protests are not the only way citizens communicate with elected officials. Americans also have a rich history of attending town halls, writing letters to elected officials and signing petitions.

Despite the variety of ways citizens can express what they want their elected officials to do, most citizens believe that politicians, and especially Congress, are failing in their roles as the public's representatives.

Cynics, as well as some scholars, suggest that taking political action may be irrelevant or simply pales in comparison to the more powerful influence of money in politics. After decades of increasing income inequality in the U.S., and growing amounts of special-interest money helping to fund election campaigns, a common finding in recent research is that elected officials respond to the opinions of the wealthy more than to those of the poor.

But other research suggests that members of Congress respond to more than just the power of money. That research found that members of Congress respond more to voters in their districts than to nonvoters when making policy. Knowing that, it seemed reasonable to ask whether elected officials in Congress respond to political activism in the same way.

Founders' Faith Affirmed

Our survey looked at four issues that were on the congressional agenda in 2012, a year for which good data is available. The issues were the repeal of the ACA, approval of the Keystone Pipeline XL, the repeal of "don't ask, don't tell," which would allow gays to serve openly in the armed services, and approval of the Korean Free Trade Agreement, which would remove tariffs on trade between the U.S. and South Korea. We asked survey respondents what their preferred policy was and then compared that to votes their members of Congress cast.

On two of these issues, we found that elected leaders' choices on roll call votes aligned better with voters in their districts compared to nonvoters. Those issues were the ACA and Keystone Pipeline.

For the ACA, activists and donors, especially activists and donors of the same party as their representative, also enjoyed greater similarity with their representatives than non-activists and non-donors.

For the Keystone Pipeline, donors were also better represented than non-donors.

So—especially for the ACA—activists were better represented by their elected officials than non-activists.

Activism pays on high-profile issues

These striking findings led us to another question: Was the power of activism strong enough to counter the influence of money?

Among voters who are not politically active in additional ways, we found that those who have the highest income are better represented than those with the least income. But activism changes this: When the poor become politically active in addition to voting, they are represented about the same as the wealthy.

This effect held true only for the ACA, not for the other issues we studied.

We believe that the effectiveness of activism directed toward House members is likely restricted to high-profile issues that are well-covered by the media, where partisan positions are strong and well-established and the issue itself is highly contentious to the public. In these circumstances, activist citizens can potentially have a stronger influence than the wealthy over the policies Congress produces.

Our findings lead us to two more observations.

First, activism may be more effective in competitive congressional districts, where elections are often won by small margins.

Voter turnout in these competitive districts is a common topic of discussion and it is often used as a political strategy to win the election. Political engagement beyond Election Day is less discussed, yet perhaps just as important.

Second, in the House of Representatives, where many claim "all politics is local," we expected to find that members are more responsive to citizen activism on a wider set of issues than the ACA. Perhaps this is true in state legislatures and city councils, where elected officials have smaller and often more homogeneous districts to represent, and where issues may not be so partisan.

In any case, the founders' faith in the power of citizen activism has been borne out, at least partially. Elected officials do respond to citizens who do more than vote — and they also respond to those activists in a way that might well counter the advantages of the wealthy in American politics.

Periodical and Internet Sources Bibliography

The following articles have been selected to supplement the diverse views presented in this chapter.

Bruce Berlin, "America's Political System Thrives on Corruption," *HuffPost*, 26 March 2017. https://www.huffpost.com/entry/ americas-political-system-thrives-on-corruption_b_58d55629e4 b0f633072b371f.

Ryan Cooper, "The Astonishing Corruption of American Democracy," *The Week*, 3 May 2018. https://theweek.com/ articles/770962/astonishing-corruption-american-democracy.

David Leonhardt, "Throw the Crooks Out: Democrats and Republicans Agree, Corruption Ails the Country," *The New York Times*, 21 June 2019. https://www.nytimes.com/2019/06/21/ opinion/corruption-trump-democrats-2020.html.

Andrew O'Hehir, "Doomed, Delusional, Divided, and Corrupt: How the Democratic Party Became a Haunted House," *Salon,* 22 September 2019. https://www.salon.com/2019/09/22/doomed-delusional-divided-and-corrupt-how-the-democratic-party-became-a-haunted-house/.

George Packer, "The Corruption of the Republican Party," *The Atlantic*, 14 December 2018. https://www.theatlantic.com/ ideas/archive/2018/12/how-did-republican-party-get-so-corrupt/578095/.

Ed Pilkington and Sabrina Siddiqui, "Democrats Go After Political 'Dark Money' with Anti-Corruption Measure," *The Guardian*, 14 February 2019. https://www.theguardian.com/us-news/2019/ feb/13/political-funding-dark-money-anti-corruption-trump.

David Von Drehle, "Our Political Parties Aren't too Powerful. They're Not Powerful Enough," *The Washington Post*, 2 October 2018. https://www.washingtonpost.com/opinions/our-political-parties-arent-too-powerful-theyre-not-powerful-enough/2018/10/02/ fac1f36c-c673-11e8-9b1c-a90f1daae309_story.html.

Kevin D. Williamson, "Bring Back Political Parties," *The National Review*, 5 November 2017. https://www.nationalreview. com/2017/11/dnc-corruption-shows-how-political-parties-should-work/.

OPPOSING
VIEWPOINTS®
SERIES

CHAPTER 3

Would the United States Benefit from a Multi-Party Political System?

Chapter Preface

After looking at the many ways the US two-party system is dysfunctional, it may seem that the obvious solution would be to move to a system with a viable third party, or with multiple parties. Several of the viewpoints in this chapter argue for just that. However, others point out that the solution is not so simple.

For one thing, you will see that the US political system—the way candidates are elected—is designed in such a way as to make it exceedingly difficult for a third party to gain any traction, even if a great many voters support it. In addition, the US party system has worked tolerably well for the bulk of the nation's history. Our current dysfunction may not, say some authors, be due to structural factors, but to the increasing diversity of the population. Some argue that the US population is simply too fragmented for the compromises needed for multiple parties to govern.

Still other viewpoints in this chapter make the case that the lack of any viable parties other than the Democrats and the Republicans has strangled the democratic process and that the only solution is the emergence of political parties that can have some electoral success. The issue is particularly important for Millennials who, according to some data cited in this chapter, have views that do not neatly align with the traditional positions of either party. The result of parties that do not truly reflect the views of the majority of Americans is that more and more citizens will become disengaged and stop voting.

And one article simply explains the structure and history of the US two-party system and hopefully clears up any confusion created by terminology used in some of the other discussions.

The first viewpoint gets the discussion off to a lively start by arguing that what is needed is not more parties, but a stronger two-party system. In fact, a smoothly functioning democratic government depends on what many people would see as *less* democracy.

> *"If the test of party strength is the ability to pass legislation, then American parties are anemic."*

US Political Parties May Be *Too* Democratic

Daniel DiSalvo

In previous chapters, several authors have raised the alarm that the practices of political parties are damaging democracy. In the following viewpoint, Daniel DiSalvo argues that democracy is not in trouble; rather, political parties are. According to this viewpoint, a strong two-party system is necessary to a well-functioning democracy, and the parties in the US are anything but strong. Daniel DiSalvo is professor and chair of political science at the City College of New York and senior fellow at the Manhattan Institute for Policy Research.

As you read, consider the following questions:

1. What sorts of political changes did social movements of the 1960s and '70s lead to?
2. What is the Westminster model as described here?
3. How does the author support his rather counterintuitive claim that less democracy at the grassroots level would lead to a more democratic government?

"Too Much Democracy?" by Daniel DiSalvo, Manhattan Institute for Policy Research, March 1, 2019. Reprinted by permission.

Observers of the current political scene warn that liberal democracy is in crisis, and that fascism or authoritarianism lurk around the corner. Contrary to such dire predictions, Frances McCall Rosenbluth and Ian Shapiro, distinguished political science professors at Yale, argue that it isn't democracy that's in crisis, but rather, political parties. Rosenbluth and Shapiro point to the paradoxical truth that "hierarchical parties are vital for a healthy democracy." Since the 1960s, social movements have sought "decentralizing" reforms to bring politics closer to the people. Changes have included the adoption of primaries and local caucuses to choose candidates, as well as direct-democracy measures, such as the initiative and referenda, to let citizens vote directly on public policy. Rather than increase satisfaction with government, however, devolving politics to the grassroots has increased "voter alienation" and fed "political dysfunction," the authors argue, while weakening the ability of the parties to mediate between citizens and government.

Against these trends, Rosenbluth and Shapiro argue that the best system is one with two big, disciplined, hierarchical, and competitive parties. This "Westminster model," with its roots in England, is characterized by single-member districts, first-past-the-post elections, and the delegation of power from members of Parliament to the party leadership. Rosenbluth and Shapiro see the Westminster model as best designed to produce "policies that serve the long-run interests of most voters" because under its terms, the parties campaign in competitive elections on clear platforms written by leaders who have the power to enact those platforms into law—should they win.

Two-party systems create durable relationships with voters, with party identifications becoming "more like marriages," the authors say; by contrast, weak-party or multiparty systems produce coalitions that act "more like hookups." Voters can express their preferences at the ballot, but they have no idea what coalition of parties will form the government after the election or the mix of policies that it will pursue. "Parties that are broad-gauged, encompass an electoral majority, and disciplined enough to enforce majority-enhancing deals," the authors conclude, "are as good as we can get in a democracy."

Like the United Kingdom, the United States has two big parties. But the authors worry that today's Republican and Democratic parties are too weak. The misguided reforms of recent decades have something to do with that weakness, but so does the U.S. Constitution. An independently elected president, staggered electoral cycles, federalism, and bicameralism prevent the concentration of political power. Consequently, though members of each party regularly vote together in Congress, creating the appearance of unity and discipline, American parties have "great difficulty coalescing around programmatic policies, and even greater difficulties in implementing them." Party unity on roll-call votes has more to do with political positioning to fend off primary challenges than with crafting public policy. If the test of party strength is the ability to pass legislation, then American parties are anemic. Most laws passed in Washington receive substantial bipartisan support—and bipartisanship is just "another label for deal making in the absence of a clear partisan program." Voter frustration is predictable in a system where primaries push candidates to the extremes but the imperatives of legislating force them to the center, and even into compromises with the other party.

Yet multiparty systems elsewhere show little evidence of being a better alternative. Rosenbluth and Shapiro contend that what is commonly regarded as the strength of Nordic countries' multiparty, proportional-representation systems—that they enhance representation at the ballot box—may instead be a drawback. Without cultural unity and economic prosperity, such systems can easily fragment, leaving openings for extremists on the left and right. Nordic party systems owe their success to a confluence of events in the postwar years that produced "manufacturing-based prosperity sufficient to fund both job stability and generous social insurance." Since then, however, declines in manufacturing employment and increased immigration "may have pulled the lynchpin that held that Jenga tower in place." In proportional-representation systems, they contend, deindustrialization and mass migration lead to party fragmentation, opening the door to chauvinistic populism.

Germany's party system is a hybrid, based on a combination of proportional lists and single-member districts, but it too seems likely to struggle with the decline of manufacturing employment. As the number of workers with good jobs has shrunk, a growing group of marginalized workers seeks more radical political options. "The danger," the authors warn, "not only for Social Democrats but for all of Germany, is that once unions fall below a critical mass, the cohesion of the German left gives way." And without the discipline of a party organization to hold things in place, "disaffection can easily move far left as far right."

Rosenbluth and Shapiro rightly warn that we should be "worried by the trend in many democracies to weaken the intermediary role of political parties." Reforms designed to encourage political participation, enhance representation, and facilitate direct democracy have made matters worse. They are correct to highlight the tendency to destroy political parties from within by trying to "improve" them because "voters see the results of weak parties and respond by seeking to weaken them further."

Some of their arguments deserve some skepticism, though. It's dubious that "good public policy" should be the sole criterion on which to evaluate a party system. Rosenbluth and Shapiro see Britain as a "well governed country," with "national health insurance, good public education, environmental protection, and economic dynamism." If only America had stronger parties, then it, too, could have the National Health Service, they write—not a prospect that everyone will find enticing. And the U.S. might need to give up on the Constitution to do it.

Rosenbluth and Shapiro assume that they know what "good policy" is, but their arguments show a troubling circularity, in which the "long run interests of most voters most of the time" turns out to align with the familiar "market capitalism with a robust welfare state." But hasn't such policy centrism contributed to our current predicament? Whether their suggested reforms could gain any traction is unclear at best. They concede that "reversing changes that were adopted in the name of democracy is hard," but that's an understatement. In the U.S. such efforts run headlong into constitutional barriers. And regardless of the wisdom of some of their proposals, almost all of them run counter to the contemporary egalitarian spirit and would quickly be labeled elitist, anti-democratic, unrepresentative—or worse.

Unfortunately, Rosenbluth and Shapiro's call for reformers to give up on current decentralizing strategies is likely to fall on deaf ears. The "problem" with democracy is that it democratizes—even to the point of destroying the conditions for its functioning. This would explain why so many people in Western democracies seem more willing to give up on democracy entirely than to endorse reforms that could be labeled un-democratic. Nonetheless, Rosenbluth and Shapiro make a powerful case for why we should favor big, strong political parties to maintain a healthy democracy.

> *"If voters do not have meaningful choices at the ballot box, why should they bother to show up?"*

A Multi-Party System Is Necessary for a True Democracy

George Cheung

In the previous viewpoint, the author argued that a two-party system with strong, hierarchical parties was necessary for an effective democracy. In the following viewpoint, George Cheung disagrees. Cheung says that you can't have a true democracy in such a system. A multi-party political system is necessary not only to give more people a voice in government, but a wider array of choices in candidates is also necessary to increase voter turnout. George Cheung is program director for the Joyce Foundation's Democracy Program.

As you read, consider the following questions:

1. How does the author characterize Millennial voters?
2. What is proportional representation, and why is it necessary for a multi-party system to be effective?
3. According to the viewpoint, what sorts of compromises does the two-party system force upon voters?

"Strengthening Democracy by Embracing a Multi-Party System," by George Cheung, Stanford Social Innovation Review, February 4, 2016. Reprinted by permission.

P ro-democracy reformers, activists, and funders in the United States tend to focus on increasing voter turnout by decreasing the barriers to voter registration and casting a ballot. But in doing so, they're missing something important: the broken two-party system. In the market economy consumers have a plethora of choices for virtually every good and service. How, then, when it comes to US general elections, can one expect the American voter to be excited with two choices at best—or, as in most Congressional and many state legislative races, no meaningful choice at all?

Reducing barriers to voting is a good idea, but what's really needed is a shift to a multi-party system through proportional representation; many comparative studies suggest that such a shift would lead to an increase in voter turnout of between 9 and 12 percent.

Young People Want More Choices

As a generation, Millennials are more ethnically diverse, hold more progressive views on social issues, and are more likely to favor a strong role for government than previous cohorts. How does this translate into affiliating with political parties? A poll conducted by the Pew Research Center in early 2014, found that about half of Millennials did not identify with either the Democratic or Republican political party, an increase from 38 percent in 2004. Further, only 31 percent of Millennials saw big differences between the two parties, compared to 43 percent of all respondents in the same survey.

These data suggest a desire for alternative choices. In a NBC News/Survey Monkey poll of Democratic voters released in mid-October, 2015, 54 percent of young people backed socialist Bernie Sanders compared to just 26 percent for Hillary Clinton. Under a proportional representation system, many of these young people might gravitate towards a Social Democratic, Green, or Working Families Party. Without any significant change to the US electoral system, we should expect continued political disaffection by young

COKE OR PEPSI?

Third parties face many obstacles in the United States. In all states, the Democratic and Republican candidates automatically get on the ballot, whereas third-party candidates usually have to get thousands of signatures on petitions just to be listed on the ballot. The state and federal governments, which make rules governing elections, are composed of elected Democratic and Republican officials, who have a strong incentive to protect the existing duopoly. Also, third-party candidates often face financial difficulties because a party must have received at least 5 percent of the vote in the previous election in order to qualify for federal funds.

The two political parties are a lot like the two giants of the cola world, Coke and Pepsi. Although each wants to win, they both recognize that it is in their mutual interest to keep a third cola from gaining significant market share. Coke and Pepsi, many people have argued, conspire to keep any competitor from gaining ground. For example, in supermarkets, cola displays at the end of the aisles are often given over to Coke for six months of the year and Pepsi for the other six. Competitors such as Royal Crown face an extremely difficult challenge. The Democrats and the Republicans function in much the same way.

"Third Parties," Spark Notes.

people, barring the exceptional presidential candidate who is able to inspire and mobilize.

Strategic Voting, the Spoiler Effect, and the GOP Civil War

"But we have lots of political parties." That's what one Democratic Party activist told me in a recent conversation about the merits of a multi-party system. He was technically correct; however, the US electoral system, often called "first past the post" or "winner-take-all" system, inherited from British colonialism, is set up to give just two parties any meaningful chance to win elections and govern. In the United States, voters who favor a non-major party candidate must decide between casting a strategic vote for the "lesser of two evils" or casting a vote for their first choice, which could perversely help their least favored candidate to win. (Meanwhile, the vast majority of democracies in other countries have adopted true multi-party systems, mostly as a way for elections to truly reflect the views of voters.)

Consider how current non-major parties have fared in recent US elections. On the left, the Working Families Party arguably has the most momentum. Launched in 1998 by a coalition of labor unions, community-based organizations, and remnants of the New Party, the Working Families Party is electorally active in a handful of states. In New York, where fusion voting allows two or more political parties on a ballot to list the same candidate, the party has been able to claim victories of endorsed candidates including Governor Andrew Cuomo and New York City Mayor Bill de Blasio. However, only one candidate, Edwin Gomes, has ever been able to win election solely as the nominee of the Working Families Party; the race was for State Senate in Connecticut, and Gomes had formerly represented the same district as a Democrat.

Without a change to the electoral system, the Working Families Party will struggle to win a single seat in any legislative chamber—that's a far cry from being able to channel energy from protest movements such as Occupy Wall Street into electoral power.

On the right, there's the very different dynamic of the Tea Party. Since the 2008 elections, Tea Party candidates do not run under the party label. Instead, they typically challenge establishment Republicans by offering what they tout as a more ideologically pure alternative. Successful Tea Party house candidates have formed the Freedom Caucus, which generally blocks the Republican Caucus from compromising with Democrats. Under a multi-party system, the Tea Party could function as a separate party, distinct from the pro-business, pro-immigration Republican Party of previous generations. That structure would not necessarily increase voter turnout among conservatives, but it could very well result in a more functional Congress where compromise is not taboo.

Increasing Competition and Enhancing Voting Rights

The lack of competitive races is a sad hallmark of the US electoral system. In most states, the decennial process of redistricting results is effectively an incumbency protection plan. Races, at least in the general election, are largely pro forma. I've voted in four states since first registering in 1991. I can recall voting in only one Congressional election where the incumbent didn't win in a landslide.

Elections in a multi-party system are structurally more competitive. With single member districts in a two-party race (districts that elect one representative to office), a candidate needs 50 percent plus one vote to win a seat. In three-member districts (which were used to elect the Illinois State Assembly for more than 100 years, until 1980), the threshold for winning one of three seats can be 30 percent or even less. A shift to multi-member districts (where more than one person is elected to office) could make virtually every district competitive, forcing all candidates to campaign aggressively and encourage voters to participate.

What's more, the increase in competitiveness would not come at the expense of voting rights. Since voters who support Democratic congressional and state legislative candidates are more concentrated in urban areas, more competitive races would mean splitting up these communities and combining them with predominantly Republican suburbs. Given that these urban communities are disproportionately composed of people of color, such a change could have a detrimental impact on minority voting rights—a difficult tradeoff. A multi-member district system could resolve the tension by offering meaningful competition but also providing a method for communities of color to elect someone of their choice. In fact, for Asian Americans, who do not have the same history of racial segregation as African Americans, a multi-member district system offers an opportunity to more easily elect their preferred candidate.

Modernizing our system of election administration is critical to removing barriers to participation and instilling confidence that each vote will be counted. But if voters do not have meaningful choices at the ballot box, why should they bother to show up?

> *"I think the healthiest thing would be to try to figure out ways to remind members of both parties in Congress that their jobs are to make policy and govern this country, not just serve their constituents or voting base or party elites."*

US Political Problems Are More Complex Than Just a Lack of a Meaningful Third Party

Sarah Shair-Rosenfield

In the following viewpoint Sarah Shair-Rosenfield addresses questions such as how likely it is that a third party could ever gain power in the United States, public versus party views of potential coalition governments, the duty of political parties, and whether or not current political parties in the United States are fulfilling their obligations. This viewpoint takes the form of a question and answer session. Sarah Shair-Rosenfield is a professor in Arizona State University's School of Politics and Global Studies. Her research focuses on the politics of electoral reform.

"Would America Benefit from a Three-Party Political System?" by Sarah Shair-Rosenfield, Arizona State University, November 6, 2017. Reprinted by permission.

As you read, consider the following questions:

1. What is Duverger's Law?
2. Could the United States form a coalition government if the parties wanted to, according to the viewpoint?
3. How does Sarah Shair-Rosenfield describe the job of political parties in Congress? Does she believe the parties are doing their jobs?

Not since the 1960s has the United States been so divided, largely split into two political camps.

But what if a third major political party emerged in the U.S.? Would it lead to more nuanced political discourse? Is a third major party even possible, or is the two-party system "baked in" to the United States' existing election laws and legislative rules?

ASU Now spoke with Sarah Shair-Rosenfield, a professor in Arizona State University's School of Politics and Global Studies whose research focuses on the politics of electoral reform, to discuss this possibility.

Question: How likely is it for a three-or-more-party system to emerge in this country at some point?

Answer: It is difficult to predict, though the odds are not high. It's easy to assume that voter practices and norms surrounding elections—that people typically vote for either Democrats or Republicans—are the reason for this. But the actual electoral rules structuring congressional elections are one of the main sources of why the two-party system remains so strong.

We have what are called "winner take all" electoral districts for Congress: Every electoral district (House and Senate) has one seat available, and the winner is the person who gets the largest number of votes in that district, even if that number isn't a majority. This type of system nearly always produces two major parties—political scientists refer to this as "Duverger's Law." This is true

ADVANTAGES AND DISADVANTAGES OF THE TWO-PARTY SYSTEM

A two-party system is when a country's politics is dominated by two major parties. One party usually holds the majority in government while the opposition is called the minority party. Other parties do exist in most two-party systems, but there are only two major parties that dominate government. In the U.S., that would be the Republican and Democratic parties.

- In a two-party system, the parties involved compete to present information to their voters in a way that is easy to understand. With only two major parties that have a clear chance of winning the elections, it is also easier for voters to make a choice.
- Because the parties are so big, in a two party system, the parties have to represent the wide range of views and interests of the public in order to keep earning votes.
- Two party systems are more stable, with many loyal voters sticking to one of the two parties, which prevents a sudden shift in balance when political trends arise.
- Unlike one-party systems, two party systems are often more democratic, encouraging the public to take part in elections.

The disadvantage of having only two major parties in government is that the government will be subject to the weaknesses of those two parties. Candidates are self serving and often only represent certain special interests.

"Two Party System Definition," History on the Net.

even if third parties occasionally are able to break through in seat victories in a few districts, like when Green candidates do really well in elections in particular cities. This effect is compounded by the fact that there are really very few limits on campaign finance contributions and fundraising. This favors existing parties and incumbent candidates, so smaller parties may at best see only limited gains in the long run.

Q: Is our government able to deal with something akin to what we see in other countries where a third or fourth party may hold substantial numbers of seats?

A: To my knowledge, there's nothing in the Constitution or enabling legislation that prevents a coalition government from forming in the U.S. If a third party emerged, like a Progressive Left or a separate Tea Party, and their candidates won House or Senate seats, there isn't anything keeping them from caucusing with the Democrats or Republicans to form a majority to pass laws or joining the cabinet of a Democratic or Republican president to put those laws into practice.

But the big challenge for a multi-party U.S. Congress is the fact that the U.S. has what scholars of comparative politics would call relatively "undisciplined" legislative parties. In other words, while many other countries' legislatures have either formal or informal rules in place to encourage or force party members into voting on bills along party lines, the U.S. Congress has little in comparison. That means that individual U.S. legislators can basically vote on bills as they please from issue to issue, rather than having to vote with their co-partisans. While such individuals might be portrayed or viewed as "defectors" or "traitors" on those issues by their national party leaders, they might also come across to their constituents as "sticking to their principles." Without other penalties or incentives in place to keep them from voting against their own party, this individualistic aspect of U.S. legislative behavior sometimes makes it difficult for even two parties to come to consensus and govern.

It isn't clear how adding a third or fourth party would really affect this, since those parties presumably wouldn't have any more "disciplined" members in Congress. I guess the point is that ungovernability in Congress doesn't necessarily stem just from having two parties who rarely see eye-to-eye on policy.

Q: Have we seen the successful rise of an outside third or fourth party anywhere in the world?

A: The most notable are in the United Kingdom and Canada, which both have similar electoral rules as the U.S. has, including "winner take all" electoral districts for their national legislatures. Both historically have had two parties at any given time. However, both have also had successful third and fourth parties to varying degrees since the mid-20th century. In both cases those parties had to compete for decades to make big enough gains and establish themselves as viable opponents and coalition partners.

Q: In your opinion, would it be healthier for this country to have a three-party structure given how divisive we've become as a nation?

A: I think it's pretty clear from recent U.S. elections that a lot of people are unhappy with what they see as the status quo of the Democratic and Republican party platforms and policies. I do think that if both parties faced viable challengers, it would probably force them to more seriously reevaluate their current policy preferences and strategies, though whether they would actually change what they do once in office might be more limited. (What parties do to get elected versus what they do once they are in office is rarely the same thing.) But I'm not sure that simply adding another party or two would solve a lot of the problems of political polarization we've seen in the U.S. in recent years. I say this because a lot of other countries with rising polarization in the electorate have more than two political parties, so it's pretty clear that having more parties doesn't necessarily reduce the potential for more fixed or extreme political positions to emerge.

I think the healthiest thing would be to try to figure out ways to remind members of both parties in Congress that their jobs are to make policy and govern this country, not just serve their constituents or voting base or party elites. That doesn't really have anything to do with how many parties there are; that has to do with the kinds of individuals we elect as well as the fact that there will always be another election they are looking forward to.

> *"One reason why independents are independent is because neither political party has been able to solve the problem of social transition in America. The problem isn't so much an economic one as one of social ideology—the old question of what sort of values the country should stand for."*

Both of the Major Parties in the United States Are Losing Voters

Lawrence Davidson

So far in this chapter, the viewpoints have focused on the politics and effectiveness, or lack thereof, of the two-party system. In the following viewpoint, Lawrence Davidson takes a closer look at the specific fissures within the two major US parties, the Republicans and Democrats. Both parties, according to Davidson, lead to a complex and potentially catastrophic (at least to the parties themselves) restructuring of the landscape of American political affiliations. Lawrence Davidson is professor of history at West Chester University in West Chester, Pennsylvania.

"Political Fragmentation on the Homefront," by Lawrence Davidson, Counterpunch, September 19, 2018. Originally appeared at https://www.counterpunch.org/2018/09/19/political-fragmentation-on-the-homefront/. Reprinted by permission.

As you read, consider the following questions:

1. What are the four major political "groupings" described in this viewpoint?
2. What examples does the author give for his claim that the Democratic leadership is "out of touch"?
3. What does the author mean by "rump" party, and what, in his viewpoint, destroyed the Republican Party?

The United States is politically fragmenting. It would seem that the various cultural and ideological stresses impacting the nation are destabilizing the country's two traditional political parties.

At this point in the fragmentation process we can identify four political groupings. They are (1) those of Democratic Party persuasion—and it should be noted that the Democrats are being stressed by contesting interpretations of just what the party stands for; (2) those of continuing Republican Party persuasion, which by now really represents a small "rump" party of Trump supporters; (3) the independents now bolstered by what once was the "moderate" multitude of the Republican Party as well as a growing number of ex-Democrats on the disaffected left; and (4) the mass of apolitical Americans who have always been alienated from politics and usually do not vote. This last group also may well be growing. Let's look at these four groups in more detail against the backdrop of contemporary events.

Democratic Party Under Stress

There are reported to be some 43 million registered Democrats in the U.S. We know, however, that the Democratic Party has been having trouble translating their numbers into continuous electoral success. Why so? Part of the answer has to do with the fact that the party leaders concentrate on recruiting and satisfying a constituency of centrists. This not only leaves the leftists consistently frustrated, but also often disappoints ordinary liberals. One problem with this strategy is that the Democrats have to compete for that center element with Republicans, who are out to recruit the same centrist voters. The resulting split vote often leaves the Democrats as electoral losers. Of course, the moderate Republicans are now politically adrift, but that does not mean they will become Democrats. As we will see, they have at least one other option.

Another major problem with today's Democratic Party is its stagnant leadership. The leaders who represent the party machine—Nancy Pelosi in the House of Representatives and Charles Schumer in the Senate—are products of the traditional political scene described above. They are rhetorically stuck on the theme of broadening the middle class through the creation of an ever better economy. However, economies by their very nature not only expand but also contract. New concerns such as resurgent racism (embraced by many older middle-class white men) and the threat of ecological disaster seem beyond their political awareness. And, their ability to deal with backlashes due to issues such as abortion, drugs, immigration, LGBTQ rights and the like have been ineffectual. Thus the present Democratic leadership is out of touch and has been proven incapable of responding to the country's shifting domestic social problems. As far as foreign policy goes, both Democratic leaders are ignorant and have lost sight of what are real U.S. interests abroad. In Schumer's case, he has long ago sold out to the Zionists. Schumer has but one foreign policy issue that interests him—Israel.

It is against this background that Bernie Sanders mounted his rebellious opposition against Hillary Clinton (another machine politician) in 2016. It is also against this background that several long-term urban-based Democratic politicians have recently lost their primary bids to more daring and progressive challengers. For those of us who see themselves as serious leftists, this appears to be a forward-looking turn of events. However, due to an increasing number of alienated conservatives who now characterize themselves as "independents" progress in this direction might be hard to maintain.

The Rump Republicans

The Republican Party has already gone through the sort of identity crisis now challenging the Democrats. That crisis literally destroyed what was the traditional Republican Party. The process began with the rebellion of the party's once marginal Tea Party faction and has now been completed by Donald Trump's leadership coup. The result is a rump party. By the term "rump party" I mean the residual of a once larger group, many of the members of which have been pushed away by policy positions they can no longer support. In this case an extreme rightwing Republican faction captured what was a more centrist conservative organization and remade it in its own image.

This faction had long been present among the Republicans. One saw a glimpse of its potential in the 1964 presidential candidacy of Republican Senator Barry Goldwater. The rise of the Tea Party Republicans around 2008-2009 captured many of the Republican primary elections in the south and west of the country. The main interest of this faction is the dismantling of "big government." For instance, there should be no welfare—individual or corporate. There should be little or no government regulation of the private sector. Whole departments of the federal government (for instance Health and Human Services, Education, Transportation, etc.) should be shut down or privatized because when run by the government they are supposedly both inefficient and intrusive in people's lives.

One might think that this equals greater liberty, and that is certainly the Tea Party interpretation of their ends. However, the odd thing about this brand of rightwing "liberty" is that it is quite compatible with certain expressions of fascist authoritarianism. For instance, most Tea Party politicians take a hard, punitive position on immigration policy. There isn't a lot of concern about police brutality against minorities, and the movement is generally supportive of "gun rights." These positions have made an alliance, at least on domestic issues, with an authoritarian Donald Trump, easy to achieve.

However, as the Trump-Tea Party alliance became more powerful within the Republican Party, numerous traditional Republicans (for instance, those who believe that compromise between the major parties is the best way to govern) started to back away from the party. Thus, when you read that the "Trump bump has become a tsunami" because he has "a 90% approval rating with Republican primary voters and two thirds are in the 'strong approve category,'" don't take the claim at face value. You have to ask, 90 percent of what overall number? Is that overall number getting smaller and smaller? As a Brookings study tells it, "for Republicans, party identification took a sharp drop at the end of George W. Bush's second term and never really recovered. The trend seems to have taken another drop after Trump's election." It may be the case that self-identifying Republicans now represent no more than "21.6 percent of the electorate as a whole."

The Independents

The Republican Party isn't the only one losing members. The Democrats are too, just at a slower rate—at least as of now. Overall what this means is a steady rise in those who now see themselves as "independents." Forty-two percent of politically aware Americans described themselves this way in 2017. This was up from 39 percent a year earlier. The number has been generally climbing since 2009.

One reason why independents are independent is because neither political party has been able to solve the problem of social transition in America. The problem isn't so much an economic one as one of social ideology—the old question of what sort of values the country should stand for. Since the 1960s the nation has been generally transitioning from a white-ascendent, segregated, sexually straight and gender-biased place to a more racially equal, integrated, sexually open, gender-tolerant society. You would think that any decent person would see this as a good way to go. But most human beings are only decent within their acculturated group—which may well be a prejudiced one—and to hell with most others. That attitude has led to the political blowback that has brought with it the Trump presidency.

The alienation felt by independents doesn't mean that they are all liberals. While it may be true that many of them would favor greater compromise and cooperation in governing, these are not easy ends to achieve, particularly within a political culture dominated by special interests. Nonetheless, to the extent that neither the Republican Party nor the Democrat Party has the political will to advocate and practice such a strategy, they will continue to shrink in numbers. Then, new parties may be organized and/or the number of Americans who simply drop out of politics altogether—that is become apolitical—will grow.

The Apolitical

There is a sense in which being apolitical should be the default position of a majority of Americans. This follows from the fact that most folks operate in small, local environments and, if they were to develop any deep interest in politics, it too would be the local sort. This situation has to be qualified by the further fact that many U.S. citizens believe that all politics is corrupt in nature, as well as the awareness that the true movers and shakers are well-funded special interests. The end product is a citizen who is often left with a sense of powerlessness melded with disgust. Thus, in presidential elections the turnout nationwide is usually below 63 percent of eligible voters.

The apolitical sector may well grow very fast in the next decade as independents withdraw into apathy and indifference. If this happens, it is likely to hurt the Democrats more than the Republicans. That is because the Democratic machine politicians are counting on the alienated Republicans to cross the political line to their side. For better or worse, that is not the only option those people have. Most of them have been Republicans for their entire lives, and it took a narcissistic sociopath like Donald Trump to push them away. Their inclination is not to run and vote for a Democrat. It will more likely be to stay at home on election day.

And this may be only half the bad news for the Democrats. We have seen how their leadership is stuck in a status quo rut. Schumer and Pelosi are going to be more comfortable trying to cater to centrist Republicans than leftist Democrats. The more they pursue the former, the more they push the latter first into the ranks of the independents and then, barring the rise of a genuine Democratic Socialist Party, into the apolitical morass.

It is a time of fragmentation and uncertainty for both political parties. Mass electoral rejection of Trump and his "deplorable" allies might lead to the recapture of the Republican Party by "moderates," or maybe to a new party arising to give all those alienated conservatives a fresh home. Maybe the Democrats get new and dynamic leadership or maybe the old guard continues to run that party right into the ground. It is all up in the air.

And what will be the fate of the Democratic Party's left wing? Will Bernie Sanders dare sponsor a new party if, as is probable, it becomes clear that the Democrats cannot be moved to the left? And what if he does dare? Will it prove viable within the American political milieu? Well, just keep in mind who now owns the U.S. political copyright on the traditionally communist-denoting color "red." Those "red states" are Republican—a sure sign that the political scene has turned topsy-turvy here on the homefront.

| "A new political typology ... from the Pew Research Center ... finds eight distinct categories of political ideology."

Two-Party System? Americans Might Be Ready for Eight

Domenico Montanaro

The previous viewpoint took a close look at the fragmentation of the nation's two major political parties. In the following viewpoint, Domenico Montanaro calls that fragmentation a "crackup" and goes on to explain why the future of the American political system might include not only a third party, but as many as eight. Domenico Montanaro is a senior political editor and correspondent for National Public Radio (NPR).

As you read, consider the following questions:

1. The author outlines eight categories of political opinion as found by a Pew Research survey. Do you see any overlap in those categories?
2. What is meant by the phrase "political bystanders"?
3. What group, according to the survey discussed, makes up the greatest percentage of the population? Is that a significant percentage?

There is a political crackup happening in America.

There remain two major political parties in this country, but there are stark fissures within each. There seem to be roughly at least four stripes of politics today—the pragmatic left (think: Obama-Clinton, the left-of-center establishment Democrats), the pragmatic right (the Bush-McCain-Bob Corker Republican), the populist right (Trump's America) and the populist left (Bernie Sanders liberals).

But a new political typology out Tuesday from the Pew Research Center, based on surveys of more than 5,000 adults conducted over the summer, goes even deeper. It finds eight distinct categories of political ideology (nine if you include "bystanders," those not engaged with politics).

They are as follows, from most conservative to most liberal (in part based on how many of them crossover between the two major parties. It also mostly tracks with their approval of Trump):

1. Core Conservatives—13 percent of the general public

2. Country First Conservatives—6 percent

3. Market Skeptic Republicans—12 percent

4. New Era Enterprisers—11 percent

5. Devout and Diverse—9 percent

6. Disaffected Democrats—14 percent

7. Opportunity Democrats—12 percent

8. Solid Liberals—16 percent

While the Solid Liberals and Core Conservatives make up less than a third of the total population, they make up almost half of the most politically engaged. Because of that, they have an outsize influence in U.S. politics.

They are also, predictably, the most interested in the 2018 election. There's a stark drop off in interest in the midterms among any other group, and that points to yet again a midterm election where the most activist dominate and there's a drop in turnout from a presidential year.

Meanwhile, Pew also identified a sizable portion of the American population that are essentially political "bystanders." They're not engaged with politics, not registered to vote, young and majority-minority. And there's a lot of them—8 percent of the population, or roughly 20 million people.

Overall, Pew sums up its findings, in a new 150-page report, this way:

> Nearly a year after Donald Trump was elected president, the Republican coalition is deeply divided on such major issues as immigration, America's role in the world and the fundamental fairness of the U.S. economic system.
>
> The Democratic coalition is largely united in staunch opposition to President Trump. Yet, while Trump's election has triggered a wave of political activism within the party's sizable liberal bloc, the liberals' sky-high political energy is not nearly as evident among other segments in the Democratic base. And Democrats also are internally divided over U.S. global involvement, as well as some religious and social issues.

Here's how the eight groups break down:

Republican Leaners—Four Groups
1. Core Conservatives
13 percent of the country, 31 percent of Republicans, 43 percent of politically engaged Republicans

They are, as Pew describes:

- Male dominated and financially comfortable
- In favor of smaller government and lower corporate tax rates
- Of the belief that the U.S. economic system is fair—four-fifths don't believe the government can afford to do more for needy Americans and that blacks who can't get ahead are responsible for their own condition
- Believers in U.S. involvement in the global economy. You might call them "globalists."

- Not very socially conservative—a majority don't think immigrants are a burden and just over a third believes homosexuality should be discouraged by society.

And yet this group approves strongly of Trump. Fully 93 percent approve of the president's job performance, the highest of any group. It's even more than the Country First category, and you'll see why that might be surprising in the next section.

This could simply be the product of Core Conservatives being more politically engaged generally—and more likely to wear the "GOP" T-shirt.

2. Country First

6 percent of the country, 14 percent of Republicans, 14 percent of politically engaged Republicans

They are:

- Older and less educated than other Republican-leaning voters
- Unhappy with the direction of the country
- Nationalist—they believe the country is too open to immigrants and that Americans risk "losing our identity as a nation" because of it
- Protectionist—they don't like the U.S. involved around the world and they think immigrants are a burden
- Not of the belief that the government should do more to help the needy (70 percent) and they believe that blacks who can't get ahead are responsible for their own condition (76 percent)
- Socially conservative—they believe that homosexuality should be discouraged by society (70 percent)
- Populist—they're less likely than most other Republicans to believe the U.S. economic system is fair to most Americans

3. Market Skeptic Republicans

12 percent of the country, 22 percent of Republicans, but only 17 percent of the most politically engaged

They are:

- Populist—they believe banks and financial institutions have a negative effect on the direction of the country; 94 percent believe the economic system favors the powerful. That is much closer to Solid Liberals than Core Conservatives. And they do not believe that U.S. economy is fair to most – just 5 percent think so. This is a major distinction between them and the other GOP-leaning groups
- In favor of raising taxes on corporations and small businesses—the only GOP-leaning group to feel that way
- Of the belief that government can't afford to do more to help needy Americans. A strong majority (58 percent) says so, but they are the least likely Republican leaning group to feel that way.
- Of the belief that blacks who can't get ahead are responsible for their own condition.
- Fairly socially liberal—just 31 percent believe homosexuality should be discouraged by society
- Somewhat protectionist, though less than Country First Republicans—they are split on U.S. involvement around the globe

4. New Era Enterprisers
11 percent of the country, 17 percent of Republicans, 16 percent of the most engaged Republicans

They are:

- Youngest of the Republican-leaning categories, with an average age of 47
- Optimistic about the country—they are the most likely group to believe the next generation will be better off
- Pro-business and trade (they're globalists, too), of the belief that the economy is generally fair to most Americans (75 percent say so)
- Of the belief that being involved around the globe is good for markets

- Socially liberal—believing immigrants are not a burden and that homosexuality should not be discouraged by society
- Somewhat more diverse—two-thirds are white, but that's the lowest of all other GOP-leaning groups

Democratic Leaners—Four Groups

5. Devout and Diverse

9 percent of the country, 11 percent of Democrats, just 6 percent of the most politically engaged

They are:

- Majority-minority, struggling financially, older and the least educated of the Democratic-leaning categories. Just 15 percent have college degrees
- Very religious. Nearly two-thirds believe it is necessary to believe in God to be moral and have good values
- Politically mixed. A quarter are Republicans. It's the category with the most crossover.
- The strongest Democratic-leaning group to believe the U.S. should pay more attention at home than to problems overseas
- Largely pro-business and don't believe government regulation is necessary to protect the public's interest
- Perhaps unsurprisingly, it's the most pro-Trump Democratic group (though 60 percent still disapprove of him), but...
- Of the belief that government should provide safety nets like everyone having health care and that the country needs to still make changes to advance racial equality

6. Disaffected Democrats

14 percent of the country, 23 percent of Democrats, 11 percent of the most politically engaged

The label doesn't have to do with their disaffection with the Democratic Party. They actually regard the Democratic Party very favorably. But rather they're disaffected with government (most of them say government is "wasteful and inefficient"); politics generally (most believe voting does not give them a say in how government runs); and the direction of the country.

They're also:

- Majority-minority, lower educated, financially stressed—and fairly young (with an average age of 44)
- Anti-Trump, pro-social safety net and believe the U.S. needs to continue making changes to affect racial equality.
- Split, however, on whether hard work can help you get ahead
- Not of the belief government regulation is necessary to protect the public interest
- Of the belief that the U.S. should pay more attention to problems at home.

7. Opportunity Democrats

12 percent of the country, 20 percent of Democrats, 13 percent of the most politically engaged

They are:

- Majority white and working-to-middle-class, and only a third have college degrees
- Largely liberal when it comes to the role of government, strongly in disapproval of Trump and two-thirds believe the country needs to do more to give blacks equal rights to whites (though that's the lowest of the four Democratic-leaning groups), but...
- Very much in disagreement with other Democratic-leaning groups about the ability to make it in the U.S. through hard work. They believe strongly that you can. But they are not protectionist. They believe in global engagement.

8. Solid Liberals

16 percent of the country, 33 percent of Democrats, 25 percent of the most politically engaged

They are:

- Largely white, well-educated and comfortable financially

- Young (average age of only 44)
- Unified, almost unanimously in their disapproval of Trump (99 percent disapprove). And they are activist about it—half say they have contributed to a candidate or campaign in the past year. For context, just a third of Core Conservatives say the same. Four-in-10 Solid Liberals say they've participated in a protest against Trump's policies.
- Unified in their belief that government has the responsibility to make sure all Americans have health care and have a strong sense of racial justice. There is near-unanimous agreement among this group that the country needs to continue making changes to give blacks equal rights with whites
- Of the belief that hard work and determination are no guarantee of success in the United States. Nearly three-quarters of this group says so, and this is an area where they largely differ from the other three Democratic groups as well as the Republican-leaning categories.
- Strongly of the belief that it's necessary to regulate businesses to protect the public interest, another area where they differ with half of the Democratic-leaning categories and all of the Republican-leaning ones
- Very much globalists. Very few, just one-in-10, believe the U.S. should pay less attention overseas and focus more on problems at home. That is a major difference with two of the Democratic-leaning categories and three of the Republican-leaning ones
- Largely nonreligious. Just 9 percent believe it's necessary to believe in God to be moral and have good values

> *"The two-party system came into being because the structure of U.S. elections ... tends to lead to dominance by two major political parties."*

The Two-Party System Is Baked into US Politics

Lumen Learning

Throughout the viewpoints in this chapter, you have read references to the rules, structure, and history of the two-party system in US government. In the following viewpoint authors from Lumen Learning offer more detail about how that system is organized and how it operates, while not taking a particular perspective. Hopefully it will clear up any nagging questions you may have at this point. Lumen Learning is an open digital education platform.

As you read, consider the following questions:

1. What is the winner-take-all system described here, and why does it favor a two-party system?
2. By contrast, what is proportional representation?
3. What features of the US population have contributed to the lack of viable third parties?

One of the cornerstones of a vibrant democracy is citizens' ability to influence government through voting. In order for that influence to be meaningful, citizens must send clear signals to their leaders about what they wish the government to do. It only makes sense, then, that a democracy will benefit if voters have several clearly differentiated options available to them at the polls on Election Day. Having these options means voters can select a candidate who more closely represents their own preferences on the important issues of the day. It also gives individuals who are considering voting a reason to participate. After all, you are more likely to vote if you care about who wins and who loses. The existence of two major parties, especially in our present era of strong parties, leads to sharp distinctions between the candidates and between the party organizations.

Why do we have two parties? The two-party system came into being because the structure of U.S. elections, with one seat tied to a geographic district, tends to lead to dominance by two major political parties. Even when there are other options on the ballot, most voters understand that minor parties have no real chance of winning even a single office. Hence, they vote for candidates of the two major parties in order to support a potential winner. Of the 535 members of the House and Senate, only a handful identify as something other than Republican or Democrat. Third parties have fared no better in presidential elections. No third-party candidate has ever won the presidency. Some historians or political scientists might consider Abraham Lincoln to have been such a candidate, but in 1860, the Republicans were a major party that had subsumed members of earlier parties, such as the Whig Party, and they were the only major party other than the Democratic Party.

Election Rules and the Two-Party System

A number of reasons have been suggested to explain why the structure of U.S. elections has resulted in a two-party system. Most of the blame has been placed on the process used to select its representatives. First, most elections at the state and national levels are winner-take-all: The candidate who receives the greatest overall number of votes wins. Winner-take-all elections with one representative elected for one geographic district allow voters to develop a personal relationship with "their" representative to the government. They know exactly whom to blame, or thank, for the actions of that government. But these elections also tend to limit the number of people who run for office. Otherwise-qualified candidates might not stand for election if they feel the incumbent or another candidate has an early advantage in the race. And since voters do not like to waste votes, third parties must convince voters they have a real chance of winning races before voters will take them seriously. This is a tall order given the vast resources and mobilization tools available to the existing parties, especially if an incumbent is one of the competitors. In turn, the likelihood that third-party challengers will lose an election bid makes it more difficult to raise funds to support later attempts.[1]

Winner-take-all systems of electing candidates to office, which exist in several countries other than the United States, require that the winner receive either the majority of votes or a plurality of the votes. U.S. elections are based on plurality voting. Plurality voting, commonly referred to as first-past-the-post, is based on the principle that the individual candidate with the most votes wins, whether or not he or she gains a majority (51 percent or greater) of the total votes cast. For instance, Abraham Lincoln won the presidency in 1860 even though he clearly lacked majority support given the number of candidates in the race. In 1860, four candidates competed for the presidency: Lincoln, a Republican; two Democrats, one from the northern wing of the party and one from the southern wing; and a member of the newly formed Constitutional Union Party, a southern party that wished to prevent the nation from dividing over the issue of slavery. Votes were split among all four parties, and Lincoln became president with only 40 percent of the vote, not a majority of votes cast but more than any of the other three candidates had received, and enough to give him a majority in the Electoral College, the body that ultimately decides presidential elections. Plurality voting has been justified as the simplest and most cost-effective method for identifying a victor in a democracy. A single election can be held on a single day, and the victor of the competition is easily selected. On the other hand, systems in which people vote for a single candidate in an individual district often cost more money because drawing district lines and registering voters according to district is often expensive and cumbersome.[2]

In a system in which individual candidates compete for individual seats representing unique geographic districts, a candidate must receive a fairly large number of votes in order to win. A political party that appeals to only a small percentage of voters will always lose to a party that is more popular.[3]

Because second-place (or lower) finishers will receive no reward for their efforts, those parties that do not attract enough supporters to finish first at least some of the time will eventually disappear because their supporters realize they have no hope of achieving success at the polls.[4] The failure of third parties to win and the possibility that they will draw votes away from the party the voter had favored before—resulting in a win for the party the voter liked least—makes people hesitant to vote for the third party's candidates a second time. This has been the fate of all U.S. third parties—the Populist Party, the Progressives, the Dixiecrats, the Reform Party, and others.

In a proportional electoral system, however, parties advertise who is on their candidate list and voters pick a party. Then, legislative seats are doled out to the parties based on the proportion of support each party receives. While the Green Party in the United States might not win a single congressional seat in some years thanks to plurality voting, in a proportional system, it stands a chance to get a few seats in the legislature regardless. For example, assume the Green Party gets 7 percent of the vote. In the United States, 7 percent will never be enough to win a single seat, shutting the Green candidates out of Congress entirely, whereas in a proportional system, the Green Party will get 7 percent of the total number of legislative seats available. Hence, it could get a foothold for its issues and perhaps increase its support over time. But with plurality voting, it doesn't stand a chance.

Third parties, often born of frustration with the current system, attract supporters from one or both of the existing parties during an election but fail to attract enough votes to win. After the election is over, supporters experience remorse when their least-favorite candidate wins instead. For example, in the 2000 election, Ralph Nader ran for president as the candidate of the Green Party. Nader, a longtime consumer activist concerned with environmental issues and social justice, attracted many votes from people who usually voted for Democratic candidates. This has caused some to claim that Democratic nominee Al Gore lost the 2000 election to Republican George W. Bush, because Nader won Democratic votes in Florida that might otherwise have gone to Gore.[5]

Abandoning plurality voting, even if the winner-take-all election were kept, would almost certainly increase the number of parties from which voters could choose. The easiest switch would be to a majoritarian voting scheme, in which a candidate wins only if he or she enjoys the support of a majority of voters. If no candidate wins a majority in the first round of voting, a run-off election is held among the top contenders. Some states conduct their primary elections within the two major political parties in this way.

A second way to increase the number of parties in the U.S. system is to abandon the winner-take-all approach. Rather than allowing voters to pick their representatives directly, many democracies have chosen to have voters pick their preferred party and allow the party to select the individuals who serve in government. The argument for this method is that it is ultimately the party and not the individual who will influence policy. Under this model of proportional representation, legislative seats are allocated to competing parties based on the total share of votes they receive in the election. As a result, any given election can have multiple winners, and voters who might prefer a smaller party over a major one have a chance to be represented in government.

One possible way to implement proportional representation in the United States is to allocate legislative seats based on the national level of support for each party's presidential candidate, rather than on the results of individual races. If this method had been used in the 1996 elections, 8 percent of the seats in Congress would have gone to Ross Perot's Reform Party because he won 8 percent of the votes cast. Even though Perot himself lost, his supporters would have been rewarded for their efforts with representatives who had a real voice in government. And Perot's party's chances of survival would have greatly increased.

Electoral rules are probably not the only reason the United States has a two-party system. We need only look at the number of parties in the British or Canadian systems, both of which are winner-take-all plurality systems like that in the United States, to see that it is possible to have more than two parties while still directly electing representatives. The two-party system is also rooted in U.S. history. The first parties, the Federalists and the Jeffersonian Republicans, disagreed about how much power should be given to the federal government, and differences over other important issues further strengthened this divide. Over time, these parties evolved into others by inheriting, for the most part, the general ideological positions and constituents of their predecessors, but no more than two major parties ever formed. Instead of parties arising based on region or ethnicity, various regions and ethnic groups sought a place in one of the two major parties.

Scholars of voting behavior have also suggested at least three other characteristics of the U.S. system that are likely to influence party outcomes: the Electoral College, demobilized ethnicity, and campaign and election laws. First, the United States has a presidential system in which the winner is selected not directly by the popular vote but indirectly by a group of electors known collectively as the Electoral College. The winner-take-all system also applies in the Electoral College. In all but two states (Maine and

Nebraska), the total of the state's electoral votes go to the candidate who wins the plurality of the popular vote in that state. Even if a new, third party is able to win the support of a lot of voters, it must be able to do so in several states in order to win enough electoral votes to have a chance of winning the presidency.[6]

Besides the existence of the Electoral College, political scientist Gary W. Cox has also suggested that the relative prosperity of the United States and the relative unity of its citizens have prevented the formation of "large dissenting groups" that might give support to third parties.[7] This is similar to the argument that the United States does not have viable third parties, because none of its regions is dominated by mobilized ethnic minorities that have created political parties in order to defend and to address concerns solely of interest to that ethnic group. Such parties are common in other countries.

Finally, party success is strongly influenced by local election laws. Someone has to write the rules that govern elections, and those rules help to determine outcomes. In the United States, such rules have been written to make it easy for existing parties to secure a spot for their candidates in future elections. But some states create significant burdens for candidates who wish to run as independents or who choose to represent new parties. For example, one common practice is to require a candidate who does not have the support of a major party to ask registered voters to sign a petition. Sometimes, thousands of signatures are required before a candidate's name can be placed on the ballot, but a small third party that does have large numbers of supporters in some states may not be able to secure enough signatures for this to happen.[8]

Given the obstacles to the formation of third parties, it is unlikely that serious challenges to the U.S. two-party system will emerge. But this does not mean that we should view it as entirely stable either. The U.S. party system is technically a loose organization of fifty different state parties and has undergone several considerable changes since its initial consolidation after the Civil War. Third-party movements may have played a role in some of these changes, but all resulted in a shifting of party loyalties among the U.S. electorate.

Critical Elections and Realignment

Political parties exist for the purpose of winning elections in order to influence public policy. This requires them to build coalitions across a wide range of voters who share similar preferences. Since most U.S. voters identify as moderates,[9] the historical tendency has been for the two parties to compete for "the middle" while also trying to mobilize their more loyal bases. If voters' preferences remained stable for long periods of time, and if both parties did a good job of competing for their votes, we could expect Republicans and Democrats to be reasonably competitive in any given election. Election outcomes would probably be based on the way voters compared the parties on the most important events of the day rather than on electoral strategy.

There are many reasons we would be wrong in these expectations, however. First, the electorate isn't entirely stable. Each generation of voters has been a bit different from the last. Over time, the United States has become more socially liberal, especially on topics related to race and gender, and millennials—those aged 18–34—are more liberal than members of older generations.[10] The electorate's economic preferences have changed, and different social groups are likely to become more engaged in politics now than they did in the past. Surveys conducted in 2016, for example, revealed that candidates' religion is less important to voters than it once was. Also, as young Latinos reach voting age, they seem more inclined to vote than do their parents, which may raise the traditionally low voting rates among this ethnic group.[11] Internal population shifts and displacements have also occurred, as various regions have taken their turn experiencing economic growth or stagnation, and as new waves of immigrants have come to U.S. shores.

Additionally, the major parties have not always been unified in their approach to contesting elections. While we think of both Congress and the presidency as national offices, the reality is that congressional elections are sometimes more like local elections. Voters may reflect on their preferences for national policy when deciding whom to send to the Senate or the House of Representatives, but they are very likely to view national policy in the context of its effects on their area, their family, or themselves, not based on what is happening to the country as a whole. For example, while many voters want to reduce the federal budget, those over sixty-five are particularly concerned that no cuts to the Medicare program be made.[12] One-third of those polled reported that "senior's issues" were most important to them when voting for national officeholders.[13] If they hope to keep their jobs, elected officials must thus be sensitive to preferences in their home constituencies as well as the preferences of their national party.

Finally, it sometimes happens that over a series of elections, parties may be unable or unwilling to adapt their positions to broader socio-demographic or economic forces. Parties need to be aware when society changes. If leaders refuse to recognize that public opinion has changed, the party is unlikely to win in the next election. For example, people who describe themselves as evangelical Christians are an important Republican constituency; they are also strongly opposed to abortion.[14] Thus, even though the majority of U.S. adults believe abortion should be legal in at least some instances, such as when a pregnancy is the result of rape or incest, or threatens the life of the mother, the position of many Republican presidential candidates in 2016 was to oppose abortion in all cases.[15]

As a result, many women view the Republican Party as unsympathetic to their interests and are more likely to support Democratic candidates.[16] Similarly (or simultaneously), groups that have felt that the party has served their causes in the past may decide to look elsewhere if they feel their needs are no longer being met. Either way, the party system will be upended as a result of a party realignment, or a shifting of party allegiances within the electorate.[17]

There have been six distinctive periods in U.S. history when new political parties have emerged, control of the presidency has shifted from one party to another, or significant changes in a party's makeup have occurred.

Periods of Party Dominance and Realignment

ERA	PARTY SYSTEMS AND REALIGNMENTS
1796–1824	First Party System: Federalists (urban elites, southern planters, New England) oppose Democratic-Republicans (rural, small farmers and artisans, the South and the West).
1828–1856	Second Party System: Democrats (the South, cities, farmers and artisans, immigrants) oppose Whigs (former Federalists, the North, middle class, native-born Americans).
1860–1892	Third Party System: Republicans (former Whigs plus African Americans) control the presidency. Only one Democrat, Grover Cleveland, is elected president (1884, 1892).
1896–1932	Fourth Party System: Republicans control the presidency. Only one Democrat, Woodrow Wilson, is elected president (1912, 1916). Challenges to major parties are raised by Populists and Progressives.
1932–1964	Fifth Party System. Democrats control the presidency. Only one Republican, Dwight Eisenhower, is elected president (1952, 1956). Major party realignment as African Americans become part of the Democratic coalition.
1964–present	Sixth Party System. No one party controls the presidency. Ongoing realignment as southern whites and many northern members of the working class begin to vote for Republicans. Latinos and Asians immigrate, most of whom vote for Democrats.

One of the best-known party realignments occurred when Democrats moved to include African Americans and other minorities into their national coalition during the Great Depression. After the Civil War, Republicans, the party of Lincoln, were viewed as the party that had freed the slaves. Their efforts to provide blacks with greater legal rights earned them the support of African Americans in both the South, where they were newly enfranchised, and the Northeast. When the Democrats, the party of the Confederacy, lost control of the South after the Civil War, Republicans ruled the region. However, the Democrats regained control of the South after the removal of the Union army in 1877. Democrats had largely supported slavery before the Civil War, and they opposed postwar efforts to integrate African Americans into society after they were liberated. In addition, Democrats in the North and Midwest drew their greatest support from labor union members and immigrants who viewed African Americans as competitors for jobs and government resources, and who thus tended to oppose the extension of rights to African Americans as much as their southern counterparts did.[18]

While the Democrats' opposition to civil rights may have provided regional advantages in southern or urban elections, it was largely disastrous for national politics. From 1868 to 1931, Democratic candidates won just four of sixteen presidential elections. Two of these victories can be explained as a result of the spoiler effect of the Progressive Party in 1912 and then Woodrow Wilson's reelection during World War I in 1916. This rather-dismal success rate suggested that a change in the governing coalition would be needed if the party were to have a chance at once again becoming a player on the national level.

That change began with the 1932 presidential campaign of Franklin Delano Roosevelt. FDR determined that his best path toward victory was to create a new coalition based not on region or ethnicity, but on the suffering of those hurt the most during the Great Depression. This alignment sought to bring African American voters in as a means of shoring up support in major urban areas and the Midwest, where many southern blacks had migrated in the decades after the Civil War in search of jobs and better education for their children, as well as to avoid many of the legal restrictions placed on them in the South. Roosevelt accomplished this realignment by promising assistance to those hurt most by the Depression, including African Americans.

The strategy worked. Roosevelt won the election with almost 58 percent of the popular vote and 472 Electoral College votes, compared to incumbent Herbert Hoover's 59. The 1932 election is considered an example of a critical election, one that represents a sudden, clear, and long-term shift in voter allegiances. After this election, the political parties were largely identified as being divided by differences in their members' socio-economic status. Those who favor stability of the current political and economic system tend to vote Republican, whereas those who would most benefit from changing the system usually favor Democratic candidates. Based on this alignment, the Democratic Party won the next five consecutive presidential elections and was able to build a political machine that dominated Congress into the 1990s, including holding an uninterrupted majority in the House of Representatives from 1954 until 1994.

The realignment of the parties did have consequences for Democrats. African Americans became an increasingly important part of the Democratic coalition in the 1940s through the 1960s, as the party took steps to support civil rights.[19] Most changes were limited to the state level at first, but as civil rights reform moved to the national stage, rifts between northern and southern Democrats began to emerge.[20]

Southern Democrats became increasingly convinced that national efforts to provide social welfare and encourage racial integration were violating state sovereignty and social norms. By the 1970s, many had begun to shift their allegiance to the Republican Party, whose pro-business wing shared their opposition to the growing encroachment of the national government into what they viewed as state and local matters.[21]

Almost fifty years after it had begun, the realignment of the two political parties resulted in the flipping of post-Civil War allegiances, with urban areas and the Northeast now solidly Democratic, and the South and rural areas overwhelmingly voting Republican. The result today is a political system that provides Republicans with considerable advantages in rural areas and most parts of the Deep South.[22] Democrats dominate urban politics and those parts of the South, known as the Black Belt, where the majority of residents are African American.

Summary

Electoral rules, such as the use of plurality voting, have helped turn the United States into a two-party system dominated by the Republicans and the Democrats. Several minor parties have attempted to challenge the status quo, but usually they have only been spoilers that served to divide party coalitions. But this doesn't mean the party system has always been stable; party coalitions have shifted several times in the past two hundred years.

Notes

1. Robert Richie and Steven Hill, "The Case for Proportional Representation," *Boston Review*, February–March 1998, https://bostonreview.net/archives/BR23.1/richie.html (March 15, 2016).
2. International Institute for Democracy and Electoral Assistance. 2005. *Electoral Design System: The New IDEA Handbook*. Stockholm: International IDEA, 153–156, http://www.idea.int/publications/esd/upload/esd_chapter5.pdf (March 15, 2016).
3. Duverger, Maurice. 1972 "Factors in a Two-Party and Multiparty System." In *Party Politics and Pressure Groups*. New York: Thomas Y. Crowell, 23–32.
4. Jeffrey Sachs. 2011. *The Price of Civilization*. New York: Random House, 107.
5. James Dao, "The 2000 Elections: The Green Party; Angry Democrats, Fearing Nader Cost Them Presidential Race, Threaten to Retaliate," *The New York Times*, 9 November 2000.
6. Bruce Bartlett, "Why Third Parties Can't Compete," *Forbes*, 14 May 2010.
7. George C. Edwards III. 2011. *Why the Electoral College Is Bad for America*, 2nd. ed. New Haven and London: Yale University Press, 176–177.
8. Kevin Liptak, "'Fatal Flaw:' Why Third Parties Still Fail Despite Voter Anger," http://www.cnn.com/2012/05/21/politics/third-party-fail/index.html (March 13, 2016).
9. Morris P. Fiorina, "America's Missing Moderates: Hiding in Plain Sight," 2 February 2013, http://www.the-american-interest.com/2013/02/12/americas-missing-moderates-hiding-in-plain-sight/ (March 1, 2016).
10. Jocelyn Kiley and Michael Dimock, "The GOP's Millennial Problem Runs Deep," 28 September 2014, http://www.pewresearch.org/fact-tank/2014/09/25/the-gops-millennial-problem-runs-deep/ (March 15, 2016).

11. Gabrielle Levy, "'Trump Effect' Driving Push for Latino Voter Registration," *U.S. News & World Report*, 27 January 2016, http://www.usnews.com/news/articles/2016-01-27/trump-effect-driving-push-for-latino-voter-registration (March 15, 2016).

12. "Heading into 2016 Election Season, U.S. Voters Overwhelmingly Concerned About Issues Affecting Seniors, New National Poll Reveals," 26 February 2016, http://www.prnewswire.com/news-releases/heading-into-2016-election-season-us-voters-overwhelmingly-concerned-about-issues-affecting-seniors-new-national-poll-reveals-300226953.html (March 15, 2016).

13. "Morning Consult," 25 February 2016, http://www.bringthevotehome.org/wp-content/uploads/2016/02/160209-BTVH-Memo.pdf (March 15, 2016).

14. Aaron Blake, "The Ten Most Loyal Demographic Groups for Republicans and Democrats," *The Washington Post*, 8 April 2015.

15. Irin Carmon, "GOP Candidates: Ban Abortion, No Exceptions," 7 August 2015, http://www.msnbc.com/msnbc/gop-candidates-ban-abortion-no-exceptions (March 14, 2016).

16. Aaron Blake, "The Ten Most Loyal Demographic Groups for Republicans and Democrats."

17. V.O. Key. 1964. *Politics, Parties, and Pressure Groups.* New York: Crowell.

18. Thomas Streissguth. 2003. *Hate Crimes.* New York: Facts on File, 8.

19. Philip Bump, "When Did Black Americans Start Voting So Heavily Democratic?" *The Washington Post*, 7 July 2015.

20. Edward Carmines and James Stimson. 1989. *Issue Evolution: Race and the Transformation of American Politics.* Princeton, NJ: Princeton University Press.

21. Ian Haney-Lopez, "How the GOP Became the 'White Man's Party,'" 22 December 2013, https://www.salon.com/2013/12/22/how_the_gop_became_the_white_mans_party/ (March 16, 2016).

22. Nate Cohn, "Demise of the Southern Democrat Is Now Nearly Complete," *The New York Times*, 4 December 2014.

Periodical and Internet Sources Bibliography

The following articles have been selected to supplement the diverse views presented in this chapter.

Jamelle Bouie, "Howard Schultz Doesn't Understand American History: The Most Effective Third-Party Presidential Candidates Were Polarizers, Not Centrists," *New York Times*, 31 January 2019. https://www.nytimes.com/2019/01/31/opinion/columnists/howard-schultz-third-party-candidates.html.

John Burtka IV, "Will 2018 Be a Breakout Year for a Viable Third Party?" *The American Conservative*, 10 January 2018. https://www.theamericanconservative.com/articles/will-2018-be-a-breakout-year-for-a-viable-third-party/.

Lee Drutman, **"Let a Thousand Parties Bloom: The Only Way to Prevent America's Two-Party System from Succumbing to Extremism Is to Scrap It Altogether,"** *Foreign Policy*, **19 October 2019. https://foreignpolicy.com/2019/10/19/us-democracy-two-party-system-replace-multiparty-republican-democrat/.**

Steve Herman, "How Third Party Candidates Could Upset US Presidential Election," *Voice of America News*, 2 December 2019, https://www.voanews.com/usa/us-politics/how-third-party-candidates-could-upset-us-presidential-election.

Thomas Knapp, "Voters Say They Want a Third Party; They Should Vote Accordingly," *Counterpunch*, 21 November 2019. https://www.counterpunch.org/2019/11/21/voters-say-they-want-a-third-party-they-should-vote-accordingly/.

Robert Longley, "The Important Role of US Third Parties," ThoughtCo.com, 2 July 2019. https://www.thoughtco.com/importance-of-us-third-political-parties-3320141.

Micah L Sifry, "Why America Is Stuck with Only Two Parties," *The New Republic*, 2 February 2018. https://newrepublic.com/article/146884/america-stuck-two-parties.

J. T. Young, "The Democrats' Growing Threat of a Third-Party Run," *The American Spectator*, 2 September 2019. https://spectator.org/the-democrats-growing-threat-of-a-third-party-run/.

OPPOSING
VIEWPOINTS®
SERIES

CHAPTER 4

Can the United States Transcend Party Politics?

Chapter Preface

The role of political parties in the United States is complex. As we have seen, parties play a unique and not always well-defined role in the US political system. However, a political party is fundamentally an organization of people who share a basic philosophy about government and society. At times throughout the nation's history, views about how government should operate and how society should be structured have shifted and changed. Viewpoint authors in this volume have fretted that in our times the two major parties and their philosophies have polarized. They see a world in which the two parties are like sports teams—blue team and red team—competing to win rather than working to govern.

Other writers have pointed out that while the parties themselves may be polarized, the majority of the public is more in agreement than most people realize. The problem is not so much polarization, they say, as dysfunction. The US two-party system has become paralyzed, so that the major parties are unable to accomplish anything beyond winning elections and are unwilling to listen to, much less serve, the voters that put their candidates in office.

Whichever view is correct, most if not all authors represented agree that our political system, and perhaps our very nation, is in deep trouble. But the situation is not hopeless. In this chapter, the viewpoints go beyond the problem of polarization and look at ways that citizens can transcend party politics and, perhaps, take action that can heal our nation's wounds.

The authors in this chapter float ideas for ballot initiatives, grassroots collective action, nonpartisan get out the vote (GOTV) campaigns, and a renewed emphasis on what unites us rather than what tears us apart.

In its 200-plus years, the United States has weathered some difficult storms: the Civil War, the Great Depression, the Vietnam War, and many others. The viewpoints here, though they disagree on how best to do it, offer hope that we will weather this storm as well.

| "*Part of ballot measures' power is that they reflect the will of the majority perhaps even better than elected officials do.*"

Ballot Initiative Can Transcend Political Polarization

Sarah Holdernov

Upon reading the opening of this viewpoint, you may wonder why it is in this chapter rather than the chapter on corruption. The reason is that the viewpoint's opening is the story of how ballot initiatives were used as tools that not only allowed progressive politicians to free California from the grip of political corruption, but to put power back into the hands of voters. A similar approach, according to Holdernov, might work for the nation as a whole. Sarah Holdernov is a staff writer at City Lab.

As you read, consider the following questions:

1. What examples does the author offer to support her claim that ballot initiatives transcend traditional party lines?
2. Why do ballot initiatives represent the public better than do elected officials, according to the viewpoint?
3. What part of the population is more likely to go out and vote on initiatives?

"How the Ballot Initiative Can Transcend Political Polarization," by Sarah Holdernov, psmag.com, November 27, 2018. Reprinted by permission.

F or much of the late 19th and early 20th centuries, the Southern Pacific Railroad Company ruled California. Known as "the Octopus" by those who feared it, its tentacles extended across 14,000 miles of track and expertly guided the hands of the state's political leaders.

It helped that Leland Stanford, California's eighth governor, was a railman, having invested in the incipient Central Pacific Railroad. After leaving office, Stanford acquired Southern Pacific with his partners, bringing Central under its umbrella and serving as president of both. Over the course of its reign, the railroad's sweeping influence won it 11.6 million acres of federal land grants (helping it cover more than 10 percent of the state); and almost $60 million in railroad bonds.

That's until around 1910, when Hiram Johnson, a progressive firebrand, ran for the state's highest office on a promise to break up corporate collusion—and, in turn, free California from the Octopus' control. After winning, Johnson honored his word. He introduced a new legislative tool to give California voters an unprecedented level of direct democracy: the ballot initiative.

Instead of relying on politicians alone, who were susceptible to the railroad's charms, ballot measures meant Californians were able to weigh in on specific legislative priorities, like eliminating a poll tax and increasing university funding. It was true populism: belief in the rights of the people. For the first time, voters "had an opportunity to pass policies rather than having companies take control of their politicians," says Chris Melody Fields Figueredo, the executive director of the Ballot Initiative Strategy Center, that advocates for progressive ballot measures today.

California wasn't the first state to introduce the ballot initiative—Nebraska started allowing local measures in 1897, and South Dakota followed with statewide measures in 1898. But in the century since Johnson popularized the tool, ballot initiatives have become legal in more than half of U.S. states. Starting in 2006, they waned in popularity, says Josh Altic, who tracks ballot initiative activity for election database Ballotpedia. But by the

2016 election, there was a turnaround, with a record-breaking 162 making state ballots across the country. In November's midterms, at least 155 appeared in 37 states.

As they've become more commonplace, those on the right have begun to use ballot measures just as strategically as the left. It was a ballot initiative that, in 1978, capped property taxes in California, making it harder to fund schools and public services even today. It was another California measure that, in 1994, denied illegal immigrants access to public benefits (and therefore education). In 20 other states, voters banned same-sex marriage via ballot measures during George W. Bush's presidency.

And both parties have bristled as initiatives have drifted farther from their local and anti-establishment roots. "It's hard to get one of these measures on the ballot if you don't have some sort of national interest or group—or at least a wealthy backer—supporting you," Altic said. "In 2016 ... there was a lot of corporate activity and a lot of out-of-state money involved."

This year, out-of-state interests were no less central to the process. But, in a return to the ballot measure's corporate trust-busting origins, the proposals again advanced an overwhelmingly progressive agenda. Voters in three conservative-leaning states said yes to Medicaid expansion and raised the minimum wage in two others. Florida restored voting rights to ex-felons. Michigan, Colorado, and Missouri passed redistricting reform that will make partisan gerrymandering harder.

"Thinking about the birth to where we are now, it's sort of come full circle," Figueredo said. "Politicians aren't listening to the will of the people ... so the people again are rising up and using this tool."

The initiatives' leftward lean was especially pronounced when examined in contrast with the make-up of the incoming federal legislature: While the House flipped for the Democrats, Republicans maintained control of the Senate; and while the split of state majority parties got closer to parity, state leadership stayed mostly red.

That discrepancy isn't a fluke, says Scott LaCombe, a Ph.D. student at the University of Iowa who is writing a dissertation on the subject: Ballot initiatives have historically counterbalanced the actions of the states in which they're passed. "What these initiatives do is they provide a way for people to influence policy in places that they're out of power," he said. Gay marriage bans were passed even in states with deep blue legislatures at the turn of the century; and Florida's ex-felon re-enfranchisement act will take effect even as a Republican governor is sworn in. "Ballot initiatives are a way to hold the state in line with public opinion," LaCombe continued.

Indeed, part of ballot measures' power is that they reflect the will of the majority perhaps even better than elected officials do. The popular vote doesn't win the presidency—we have the electoral college to thank for that—but it can win most state-wide measures. And while partisan gerrymandering can swing a house vote by chopping up districts, all voters in every district state-wide have equal say in deciding ballot measures.

"The fact that ... you're not constrained by the artifacts and the limitations of gerrymandering is one reason why we are able to pass these initiatives in red states," said Jonathan Schleifer, the executive director of The Fairness Project, a progressive lobbying group that fought for the minimum-wage hikes.

"That's also why there's a backlash that makes it harder to put initiatives on the ballot," he continued. In Florida, for example, they raised the threshold for initiative passage to 60 percent of the vote in 2006, while many other states require only a simple majority. Other states have put strict minimums on the number of signatures needed for putting citizen-initiated measures on the ballot; or have made it easier to repeal them once they're passed. Not all pushback is an attempt to invalidate majority rule: Critics note that ballot measures, especially those that are citizen-initiated, can be damaging when poorly designed. Still, Schleifer says that absent federal action, ballot measures are the best way to increase the wages and benefits of working people. "Opponents know that when you put these policies in front of voters, they win," he said.

To that end, ballot measures have also been used to galvanize turnout. Republicans used gay marriage-related ballot measures to get their party to the polls, in the hopes they'd vote for Bush's re-election in 2004; when he won, it seemed to confirm the strategy's value. And studies have shown that states with an initiative process do garner greater voter participation, especially in mid-term years. This November's mid-term added another data point to the trend. "The thing I saw this year is people ... saw their role in our democracy in a way I haven't seen in my 15-plus years of doing this work," Figueredo said. "Voters aren't waiting for politicians anymore," Schleifer said.

And when certain ballot measures succeed, they're even more likely to have long-term ramifications on turnout. In a paper published this year, Jake Haselswerdt, an assistant professor of political science at the University of Missouri, found that states that passed Medicaid expansion saw a direct effect on increased turnout and voter registration in the next election year. Haselswerdt did not study the voter impact of minimum-wage increases specifically, but says that helping workers earn more would likely have a similar effect to Medicaid expansion.

"If your life is unstable, or if you're living in crisis, you're less likely to vote," Haselswerdt said. It follows that policies that help bring stability—like those that keep you healthy, and financially secure—equip voters with the resources to show up to the polls.

Schleifer said the results of this election also signal a bit of a breakdown in the traditional definition of who cares about "progressive" legislation. The fight for expanded health-care benefits has come to be associated with the Democratic Party in recent years (especially as Republicans fight to dismantle the Affordable Care Act and Democrats make it a campaign centerpiece); and candidates who are pro-minimum wage, pro-voting rights, and anti-gerrymandering are overwhelmingly blue. But ballot measures are unique in that there's no clear signal telling voters what party each issue is aligned with, said LaCombe, so voters can be more comfortable splitting their tickets. "The elections have become more nationalized and polarized," he said. "But the initiatives are state-specific."

Voters didn't support all of the so-called progressive measures on the ballot this year: In Arizona, Colorado, and Washington state, voters rejected environmental protection policies like carbon fees and drilling restrictions. But Republican voters did approve labor and health-care reform.

"What is surprising a little bit is the extent to which we see the same voters voting for relatively progressive policies supporting conservative candidates," LaCombe said. That may signal that the association between liberal reform and liberals isn't so simple. Nebraska Republicans voted for Medicaid expansion along with a full Republican ticket of House and Senate representatives. These may be the blue-collar voters that make up Trump's core base: conservative on social issues, but willing to raise a working-class minimum wage.

"I think passing progressive ballot measures will send a clear signal that the way to win is focusing on the two pain points of working people," Schleifer said. "A Republican can embrace a minimum wage and expanding Medicaid." And in the states where those policies won—Arkansas, Missouri, Idaho, Nebraska, and Utah—they might be wise to do so.

As state leadership becomes more unified—only Minnesota has a house and senate controlled by different parties—there are more people than ever out of power, whether Democrats in Republican states or vice-versa. To pass policies that work for them, LaCombe says, the most viable path forward may be the ballot initiative.

> *"The Bible-thumping, pro-war, free-market purist is a rare creature. So is the gun-grabbing, abortion-loving, socialist atheist. Perfect conservative and liberal stereotypes are hard to find in the real world."*

America's Polarization Has More to Do with Personal Identity Than Political Ideology

George Hawley

This viewpoint harkens back to work by Morris Fiorina, which you read about in chapter one. Here, George Hawley expands upon Fiorina's argument that the American public is not as polarized as it appears from reading news reports. The author argues that party allegiance is often more a matter of personal identity than to agreement with the policy positions of the favored party. George Hawley is an associate professor of political science at the University of Alabama.

"America's Polarization Has Nothing to Do with Ideology," by George Hawley, theamericanconservative.com, April 24, 2018. Reprinted by permission.

As you read, consider the following questions:

1. Why do partisans often disapprove of their own political parties, according to the viewpoint?
2. In what area are Americans in most agreement, according to the author?
3. If Americans are not as separated by ideology as is often said, then why are people so angry with members of the other party?

Although a seemingly simple concept, the issue of polarization has long frustrated political scientists. A superficial examination of the American political scene suggests an intensely polarized electorate, divided along partisan and ideological lines. Watching cable news, we see competing camps that have few points of agreement, with anger the dominant emotion. Yet a dive into public opinion on questions of policy tells a different story.

In 2004, Stanford University political science professor Morris Fiorina and his colleagues persuasively argued that Americans are not bitterly divided on the most contentious policy questions, that in fact Americans lack true ideological convictions. Their argument today remains as sound as ever.

The claim that most of us have a coherent bundle of ideological constraints that inform our policy preferences and voting choices has little empirical support. The number of consistent liberals and conservatives in the electorate remains very small. The Bible-thumping, pro-war, free-market purist is a rare creature. So is the gun-grabbing, abortion-loving, socialist atheist. Perfect conservative and liberal stereotypes are hard to find in the real world.

Especially on economic issues, Americans exhibit a remarkable consensus, for better or for worse. Across the partisan divide, most people endorse a form of welfare capitalism—we just disagree on the minutia of tax policy, regulation, and the strength of the social safety net.

This claim, that polarization is not occurring, seems at odds with our everyday experiences. People are angry about politics, and strongly dislike their political opponents even when they substantively agree with them on many policy questions. After countless empirical studies and debates, scholars are inching their way towards an explanation for these contradictory trends.

Part of the apparent paradox may be explained by the nature of partisanship. Rather than the result of a rational analysis of various policy positions, it may be better to think of party allegiance as an element of personal identity. This is a point that many conservatives who decry "identity politics" often miss. Party politics itself can be a form of identity politics, even if our party identifications are downstream from other elements of identity, such as race, religion, and class.

Yet this still leaves an unresolved puzzle. We know that Republicans and Democrats strongly dislike each other. But what pundits don't always like to talk about is how much partisans themselves increasingly disapprove of their own parties. Republicans are particularly unlikely to report positive emotions towards the GOP. The partisan media would like to interpret these findings as evidence that people are frustrated with their parties' lack of ideological convictions—that the GOP, for example, has become a bunch of unprincipled "RINOS" (Republicans in Name Only), and thus its conservative voters respond with frustration. Such an explanation, however, is at odds with the finding that few Republican voters are interested in principled conservatism at all.

Eric Groenendyk of the University of Memphis may have found a solution to this puzzle. In a recent article, Groenendyk offers a new explanation for how partisans' antipathy toward the opposing party can coexist with growing frustration towards their own. In his earlier book *Competing Motives in the Partisan Mind*, Groenendyk developed the "dual motivations" theory of party identification. In short, partisans have different motives for identifying with their parties, and these sometimes conflict. Because party identification is an important part of personal identity, we want to be good and loyal partisans and we feel good when our team wins. On the other hand, we like to imagine ourselves as rational beings, forming political opinions and loyalties according to our analysis of what is happening in the world.

Ideally, there should never be dissonance between the two. When our party wins elections and enjoys real power, we hope that it delivers on its promises, providing peace, prosperity, and stability. When this fails to occur, however, our two motivations are in conflict, and we can suffer psychological turmoil. From a purely rational perspective, when our party disappoints us, we should reevaluate our support for that party, becoming independent or even joining the other side. If our party identification is a crucial part of our identity, however, this is easier said than done. Party allegiance is not fixed, but it's also not something most of us abandon easily.

According to Groenendyk, we can resolve the tension between our party identifications and our frustration with our parties by increasing our antipathy toward our parties' opponents. In other words, we can justify our vote choice if we believe the opposing party is worse. This allows us to acknowledge our disgust with our parties without jumping ship.

This process results in a curious variety of polarization. Few people love their party and think it represents their interests well. Nevertheless, we increasingly hate the other option, and this is enough to keep us in our respective camps. And the more exasperated we become with our parties, the more we demonize the other side.

Using survey data over multiple election cycles, Groenendyk showed that decreasing fondness among partisans for their own parties was associated with growing hostility toward the opposition party. This did not definitively prove that his proposed psychological mechanism explains all the dynamics of polarization. However, it did make a persuasive case that his hypothesis better explained these findings than alternative theories.

Groenendyk suggested that his hypothesis could explain other curious political developments. If out-group hostility is more important to party identification than support for particular policies or ideologies, we may not actually place very many ideological demands on our parties. Defeating our enemies may be more important than advancing specific liberal or conservative agendas. According to Groenendyk: "If partisans' identities are increasingly anchored to hatred of the outparty than affection for their inparty, electoral dynamics are likely much more fluid than many accounts suggest. Thus, insurgent candidates with questionable ideological credentials (e.g., Donald Trump) may be more appealing than one might expect in the age of ideologically sorted parties."

It is not obvious how troubling we should find this possibility. These trends long predate the Trump presidency. We may pine for the days when Americans viewed electoral politics as a competition between the greater of two goods, rather than the lesser of two evils, but those days are long gone, and American democracy continues to function reasonably well. Whether this is sustainable in the long term is an open question.

> *"Organizations have historically functioned as 'schools of democracy' that shape people's civic and political identities."*

Collective Action That Can Make Tangible Improvements in People's Lives Improves Political Participation

Ethan Frey

If the electorate is not as polarized as it seems, and if the two-party system is inevitable if not ideal, then how can we transcend political divisions, both real and imagined, and work together for the common good? In the following viewpoint, Ethan Frey offers some suggestions, including an increased emphasis on collective action. Ethan Frey is program officer for the Ford Foundation, working with cities and states to find solutions to ongoing problems.

As you read, consider the following questions:

1. Why is automatic voter registration necessary but not sufficient for increased participation in elections?
2. What effect do government policies and programs, such as Social Security, have on citizen participation?
3. What is the value of organizations in increasing turnout and other forms of citizen participation?

"How to Encourage Better and More Meaningful Political Participation in the US," by Ethan Frey, fordfoundation.org, June 24, 2016. Reprinted by permission.

E very two to four years, there is a lot of conversation about how to increase voter turnout and participation in the United States. Some helpful facts resurface: Americans' affiliations with organizations that purport to represent their interests—political parties, labor unions, religious institutions, and community-based organizations—are at historic lows, as is their trust in government institutions. As such, voter participation remains low, and communities of color and poor communities are largely excluded from the political process. So the million-dollar question is, How can people participate in their communities and the political process in ways that build their sense of agency and encourage further participation?

Hahrie Han, a political science professor at the University of California, Santa Barbara, prepared a report for the Ford Foundation that puts forward a framework for doing just that. In it, she explains why and how participation can be made more:

- **Possible.** Simply put, people must be able to participate. We need to remove barriers to participation and implement policies and procedures that make it easier for people to vote.
- **Probable.** People must want to participate. It's not enough for voting to be easy; people have to want to take part.
- **Powerful.** For people to want to participate in the political process, their participation actually has to matter—it must have a tangible impact on policy decisions, and improve people's lives.

These three dimensions give us a better sense of how to assess efforts that are designed to increase people's participation and make it more meaningful.

If We Build It, Will People Come? Not Necessarily

For example, automatic voter registration (AVR) is a policy solution that seeks to address one of the biggest barriers to greater political participation—registering to vote. Recently released data from Oregon, the first state to pass AVR, shows that AVR helped increase registration rates. But by applying Han's framework, we see that changing policy to remove barriers is *necessary but not sufficient* to increase and sustain greater voter participation. Indeed, passing AVR does not guarantee that more people—especially more poor people—will vote in greater numbers. There are also concerns that AVR may not reduce persistent disparities in the electorate—because while it makes the pool of registered voters more representative of the country's diversity, it does not address voter motivation, especially within lower-income communities.

That's because AVR addresses only one of the three dimensions of participation: AVR makes voting more *possible*. But building it does not necessarily mean people will come. In fact, history tells us that policies like AVR may not transform patterns of participation or the status quo. In 1993, the national "Motor Voter" law required state governments across the US to offer voter registration to anyone who applied for or renewed a driver's license or public assistance. But a study of the law's impact showed that while it increased voter registration rates, voter turnout actually decreased by 5 percentage points in the next general election. There are plenty of other examples of how this kind of policy intervention has failed to increase participation rates in low-income communities and communities of color.

Participation Beyond the Possible

So how can policies transform political engagement to make it not only possible but also probable that people will participate?

Social Security is a good example of how policy can transform people's patterns of participation and engagement. Social Security was designed as an economic security program to reduce poverty among the elderly. But as MIT political scientist Andrea Campbell demonstrates, it also created structural incentives for the elderly to participate in politics by "(a) giving them the resources of money and free time; (b) enhancing their levels of political interest and efficacy by tying their well-being visibly to a government program;

and (c) creating incentives for interest groups to mobilize them by creating a political identity based on program recipiency." This last point is key: Social Security created the conditions for organizations like the AARP to mobilize and solidify this constituency as one of the most consistent group of voters and dominant political blocs of the later half of the 20th century.

What kinds of 21st-century policy solutions would set the stage for making the participation of communities of color and the poor more *probable* and *powerful* in our democracy? Political participation in the US has been problematic for much of our nation's history. In fact, the only time we had anything near full participation was when only white men could vote. Voter turnout declined from 79 percent of the eligible voting age population in 1896 to just 49 percent in 1920, when women gained the right to vote. In the South, voter turnout began a precipitous decline after the withdrawal of federal troops in 1877, hitting its nadir in 1920 at 22 percent, and increasing only after the passage of the 1965 Voting Rights Act. (The VRA, as many know, was effectively gutted by the Supreme Court in 2013, but there is evidence to suggest that over time its ability to translate the right to vote into political power for communities of color was somewhat diminished.) It's simply unreasonable to think we can undo centuries of structural racism and misogyny in our electoral processes simply by removing barriers to voter registration and participation.

But also, we cannot simply import lessons from the past. Organizations—both political and apolitical—have historically functioned as "schools of democracy" that shape people's civic and political identities. Although the Elks and Shriners, for example, were not expressly political organizations, they served as effective channels for white people's participation in the 19th and early 20th centuries. One could say the same about black churches for black participation, particularly during the civil rights movement. We can draw important lessons from how these historic organizations powerfully shaped people's political identities and instilled civic

WE NEED NEW WAYS FOR CITIZENS TO PARTICIPATE

Once upon a time, when communication and access to knowledge were limited, delegating the workings of democracy to elected representatives made sense. But things have changed. Today, a growing number of people not only demand, but also play, a more active role in political life through tiny participatory acts: likes, shares, petition signatures, donations.

Participation now happens with little cost or effort. And it means that a greater number of citizens—who have traditionally not participated—are becoming more politically active, or at least more open to persuasion by those that are. People have also become politically more promiscuous. Today's digitally-empowered citizens express allegiances to multiple issues, without necessarily adhering to a political organisation. They may support causes that don't traditionally fit, often without a political motivation.

If citizens are offering up a pluralistic, chaotic input into the political conversation, then there is an urgent need for new forms of participation that can make sense of it. People are disillusioned with traditional politics, but there is also a resurgence of interest in politics. The gap needs to be filled.

norms—Ziad Munson has synthesized learnings from some more contemporary and more political movements—but we also have to think about how to adapt them to the modern era.

Collective Action Is Powerful

Making participation more possible, probable, and powerful means thinking about how individual acts of participation can have the most impact in the world. Most institutions, especially government, don't respond to individual demands (unless you have a lot of money) as well as they do to collective action. So a single act of protest is relatively unlikely to result in transformational changes in the status quo.

But collective action should serve to make the whole greater than the sum of its parts. Organizations are critical parts of that equation, and we can learn even from those whose ideologies we disagree with. In his studies of the so-called pro-life movement, sociologist Ziad Munson found that "47 percent of activists at the frontlines of the movement were either pro-choice or indifferent to issues of abortion when they joined the movement." In other words, their views on abortion did not precede their participation in the movement, but were formed as a result of it. Even more interesting: Public polling consistently shows that a majority of people favor legal access to abortion, but public policy is generally headed in the opposite direction. So how has this minority perspective been able to effectively control the policy-making agenda, and have such a transformative impact on individual civic behavior and attitudes?

Applying Han's framework, one could argue that organizations that oppose abortion have created the conditions for *powerful* participation. They have created meaningful opportunities for people to participate in their community and in the political process, where these organizations (albeit representing a minority perspective) can strategically aggregate and leverage collective participation to change policy. This is in some ways similar to the role that organizations like the AARP play vis-à-vis Social Security. According to Han and other scholars, the organizations that are best able to create these conditions possess what Harvard professor Marshall Ganz calls "strategic capacity"—that is, the capacity to turn what you have (your resources) into what you want (your goals).In the 1960s, two organizations competed to organize California's 100,000 farmworkers: the better-resourced AFL-CIO Agricultural Workers Organizing Committee and the United Farm Workers (UFW), led by Cesar Chavez. Why did the UFW, which had fewer resources, succeed where the AFL-CIO AWOC failed? Some scholars think it was because the UFW had strategic capacity. Strategic capacity is not just making plans; according to Ganz it is "a function of who leaders are—their identities, networks and tactical experiences—and how they structure their interactions with each other and their environment with respect to resource flows, accountability and deliberation." So the UFW was able to devise a more effective strategy "because the motivation of its leaders was greater than that of their rivals; they had better access to salient knowledge; and their deliberations became venues for learning."

Understanding What Works—and What Doesn't

But what, ultimately, does strategic capacity consist of, and how do scholars identify and research it? In the nonprofit sector, organizational strategic capacity remains ill defined and understudied. As Han's report points out, the private sector is light years ahead of us in this area: They spend a lot of time and money trying to understand why some businesses succeed while others fail. There is unfortunately far less literature that investigates this question from a nonprofit perspective. Moving forward, developing a deeper and more holistic understanding of how to strengthen strategic capacity (along with a precise set of metrics) may help philanthropy place more value on organizations' role in creating the conditions for social change.

There is a lot we don't yet know about why increasing and improving participation is so challenging in the US—but we do know that strengthening organizations needs to be at the heart of any meaningful effort to do so. Part of the key to unlocking participation will be developing a better understanding of the nexus between probable and powerful participation. There is certainly a role for policy in this discussion, at least to the extent that policy can determine the boundaries of political constituencies. Ultimately, though, we need strong organizations that can make the leaps between individual participation and collective action, and between collective action and tangible improvements in people's lives.

"It's never been easier for the majority of US voters to get election information and cast their ballots... [but] turnout declined last year to levels not seen since World War II."

Non-Partisan "Get Out the Vote" (GOTV) Efforts May Offer the Most Hope in Increasing Voter Turnout

Kelly Born

Previous viewpoints have stressed that the only way to overcome the problems posed by political parties and their divisive nature is to increase voter turnout. In the following viewpoint, Kelly Born offers some suggestions about how to do that. Born acknowledges that there are factors outside the control of those working to improve voter turnout, such as the influence of candidates' personalities. She also admits her ideas for solutions might make a smaller impact on the problem overall. This piece is the final part of a series of articles on this topic, published by the Stanford Social Innovation Review. *Kelly Born is a program officer for Special Projects and democracy-related grantmaking at the William and Flora Hewlett Foundation.*

"Increasing Voter Turnout: What, If Anything, Can Be Done?" by Kelly Born, ssir.org, April 25, 2016. Reprinted by permission.

As you read, consider the following questions:

1   While acknowledging the importance of voter participation, what does the author say is actually more important than increased turnout?
2. What, according to the viewpoint, are some of the problems encountered by get-out-the-vote workers?
3. What role could philanthropy play, according to the author?

This series of articles has aimed to spark conversation around whether and how the social sector can make a difference in improving US voter turnout. Thirteen experts, and many commenters, have shared their views—and we've also had the benefit of studying the current primary election cycle. What have we learned?

After a long decline in US voter turnout, the turnout rate for the current primaries has rebounded to almost 30 percent—the second highest level since 1980, and only one percentage point off from the 2008 Obama high. A variety of structural factors discussed in this series have been in play, both good (e.g., improved registration) and bad (remember the long lines in Arizona?).

But perhaps as important are factors well outside of reformists' control. The level of competition in particular campaigns and the enthusiasm (or abhorrence) inspired by various candidates matters a lot. We have seen plenty of both in the nominating contests so far this year.

While these factors are harder for the social sector to influence, other levers remain—though the likely impact of most traditional voting interventions may not be high. For me, three themes stand out:

- There is no silver bullet for increasing turnout—a mix of strategies would need to be pursued, each (on their own) with incremental effects.

- Improving the representativeness of the electorate, and knowledge about policies at stake, may be a more important (and realistic) goal than dramatically increasing overall turnout.
- Primary elections routinely see lower and even less representative turnout than general elections—and therefore may offer a particularly good opportunity for philanthropy to make a difference.

No Silver Bullet

A range of structural changes could each bring about relatively modest percentage point increases, mostly in the single digits. Wendy Weiser of the Brennan Center advocates making voter registration easier, noting that "making registration portable can boost turnout by more than 2 [percentage points]," while "allowing citizens to register at their polling place on election-day increases turnout [by] typically 5 to 7 [percentage points]." Though harder to achieve, transitioning to a multi-party system with an electoral process that allocates representatives proportionally—the system in Nordic countries and others with high voter turnout rates—could encourage greater engagement in the political process, writes George Cheung of the Joyce Foundation. This could boost voter turnout between 9 and 12 percentage points—also not a huge increase, and very difficult to bring about.

Others are more skeptical. Citing half a dozen scholars' research on efforts to reduce barriers to voting (by allowing early voting and relaxing stringent absentee balloting procedures, for example), MIT's Adam Berinsky concludes, "The balance of evidence is clear: lowering the direct costs of voting does little if anything to increase turnout." Similarly, David Becker of the Pew Elections Project notes that "it's never been easier for the majority of US voters to get election information and cast their ballots… [but] turnout declined last year to levels not seen since World War II."

Other contributors argue mobilization efforts that don't require structural or legal changes. Kate Lydon of IDEO argues that we need a more nuanced understanding of why different groups are motivated (or not) to vote, and suggests that—depending on the audience—voter mobilization efforts should highlight one of three key factors influencing voting behavior: impact, convenience, or community. Contributors such as former Minnesota Secretary of State Mark Ritchie attribute much of the variation in turnout across counties to differences in community culture and values. Becker likewise emphasizes the need to examine differences between subgroups, arguing that we need a more nuanced segmentation of voters to understand the myriad barriers and disincentives that different groups face.

But Alan Gerber and Greg Huber of Yale University caution against expecting traditional get-out-the-vote (GOTV) efforts to have a significant impact on turnout. "The key messages are that (1) it is quite challenging to increase turnout and (2) commonly used interventions produce effects on turnout in the low single digits," they write. And it's worth noting that any civic education or mobilization efforts require repetition (and funding) year in and year out—meaning less of an enduring impact than structural reforms could have.

Representativeness

Improving the electorate's representativeness and understanding of policy issues may be a more important target than trying to radically increase turnout.

As noted at the series outset, philanthropy remains a drop in the bucket compared with what parties, candidates, and interest groups spend on mobilization efforts. Moreover, with the federal prohibition on electioneering by 501(c)3 organizations, there are many things nonpartisan philanthropies hoping to increase civic engagement—regardless of the election outcome—legally cannot do. Yet several contributors make a convincing case that the social sector can play an important role in areas where others are not incentivized to act. Parties and interest groups invariably focus on voters they think are going to turn out (and turn out for them). This leaves a lot of ground uncovered. Philanthropy could make a distinctive impact by helping better inform both voters and nonvoters about policy issues, helping improve the representativeness of the electorate, or increasing turnout in America's ill-attended but increasingly important primary elections, as several contributors discussed.

The population that turns out to vote often differs notably from the US population at large.

- The gap between white and black voting rates has narrowed since the 2008 elections in both presidential elections and midterms, but white Americans' turnout rate is still almost 20 percentage points higher than Asian or Hispanic turnout in both types of elections.
- Voters age 65 and older still turn out at a rate almost 30 percentage points higher than 18- to 24-year-olds.
- The turnout rate among those earning more than $100,000 to $150,000 per year remains 30 to 50 percentage points higher than the rate for those earning less than $20,000.

So, what can be done to improve the representativeness of the electorate? Professors Jan Leighley and Jonathan Nagler suggest that the best way to increase turnout and improve the representativeness of voters (whether by age, race, or income) may be by increasing the information citizens have about candidates' policy positions. Berinsky agrees, and notes that structural reforms "designed to make voting 'easier'" can actually "magnify the existing socioeconomic biases in the composition of the electorate." This skewing happens because reforms that make the act of voting easier (e.g., online voting) may help to retain people who are already engaged and inclined to vote, but do little to stimulate the unengaged, who may be more daunted by the cognitive costs of voting than the logistical ones.

Abby Kiesa and Peter Levine of Tufts University focus specifically on youth turnout, but their argument for a multi-pronged approach is as relevant for the rest of the electorate.

They recommend a combination of structural reforms (same-day registration, pre-registration programs, and a voting age of 16 or 17 for local elections), civic education to influence cultural norms, and get-out-the-vote efforts.

The Importance of Primary Elections

Our final contributors took on primary elections—a new and (almost) uniquely American invention. Most other democracies (and the United States, too, until the 1970s) rely on party leaders to develop candidate lists. But primaries (particularly Congressional primaries) play quite an important role in US politics, in part because most voters see them as so—well—unimportant. They shouldn't: Around 80 percent of Congressional districts are either solidly Democratic or solidly Republican enough to be considered "safe" for that party. That means it's the voters who participate in those districts' primaries that really decide the election. Primaries have become the de facto general elections—and in these safe districts, the actual general elections no longer matter.

Parties and candidates often have little interest in addressing this disconnect between primaries' low profile and their importance in the political process. The social sector may be able to play an important role here.

Elaine Kamarck of the Brookings Institution confirms that primary turnout remains astoundingly low: "In the hotly contested primaries of 2010 turnout averaged 7.5 percent of the voting age population." She argues for a concerted push for all primary elections to take place on the same one or two days, rather than "spread out across 15 separate days in seven months," as they currently are. That way, "the national press would be able to cover it as a major story," and voters would be more likely to be engaged with the process. Parties and candidates are unlikely to pursue this recommendation on their own, leaving the social sector uniquely positioned to act. Likewise, more concerted GOTV efforts to improve primary turnout are, Seth Hill and Thad Kousser at the University of California, San Diego, suggest, something that only the social sector or government (if pressured to act) are likely to take on in a nonpartisan way. It's worth noting, however, that although Hill and Kousser found GOTV efforts to be twice as effective in primaries as in general elections, even their impact remains small. The authors found that people who typically vote only in November, but who received a traditional GOTV mailer, voted in primaries at a rate 0.5 percentage points higher than "November-only" voters who didn't receive the mailer. (Given that only 9.5 to 10 percent of such voters participate in primaries, this meant a 5 percent increase in turnout among this group.)

Looking at all of this, I am left with a much clearer sense of the (unfortunately, generally small) impact that most traditional voting interventions yield—but also a stronger sense of where the social sector is best positioned to intervene.

The recent GOP turnout "explosion" suggests that candidate personalities and electoral competitiveness may have a much bigger effect on turnout than many structural interventions, but these factors are also nigh impossible to control. Nonpartisan opportunities to improve turnout among specific groups, or for specific types of elections, may offer more hope. And, to end on an optimistic note, voting is sticky: 30 to 50 percent of the people who turn out due to GOTV efforts in one election will continue to vote in future elections. Moreover, although much research has been done on the impact of individual interventions on turnout, there is no way of telling what the cumulative effect of structural reforms might be—perhaps more than the sum of these parts?

In the end, whatever one's views on whether government should be larger or smaller, an effective government remains the most viable mechanism for achieving social impact at scale, and getting Americans to vote for representatives who support their interests matters for any of the outcomes we care about.

> *"We can best limit intolerance of difference by parading, talking about, and applauding our sameness … Nothing inspires greater tolerance from the intolerant than an abundance of common and unifying beliefs, practices, rituals, institutions and processes."*

Healing the Nation's Divisions Will Require Promoting Our Joint Interests

Sheri Berman

In the following viewpoint, Sheri Berman explores the sociological and psychological factors that increase the political polarization and divisions in the United States. While the rifts are deep and complex, the author argues, there are ways to approach healing. This would require shifting the public's attention from what separates us to what instead unites us. Sheri Berman is an associate professor of political science at Barnard College, Columbia University.

"Why Identity Politics Benefits the Right More Than the Left," by Sheri Berman, theguardian.com, July 14, 2018. Reprinted by permission.

As you read, consider the following questions:

1. What is the "constant can't explain a variable problem" as explained in the viewpoint?
2. How, according to the author, does a perceived threat bring to the fore otherwise hidden resentments and biases?
3. What is "social sorting," and how may it have contributed to political divisions?

O ver a year into Donald Trump's presidency, commentators are still trying to understand the election and the explosion of intolerance following it. One common view is that Trump's victory was a consequence of pervasive racism in American society.

Studies make clear, however, that racism has been decreasing over time, among Republicans and Democrats. (Views of immigration have also grown more favorable.) Moreover, since racism is deep-seated and longstanding, reference to it alone makes it difficult to understand the election of Barack Obama and Trump, the differences between Trump and the two previous Republican nominees on race and immigration, and the dramatic breakdown of social norms and civility following the elections. (Social scientists call this the "constant can't explain a variable" problem.)

This does not mean racism is irrelevant; it matters, but social science suggests it does in more complicated ways than much commentary suggests.

Perhaps because straightforward bigotry has declined precipitously while more subtle, complex resentments remain, understanding how intolerance shapes politics requires examining not just beliefs, but also the relationship between beliefs and the environments people find themselves in. This distinction has important implications for how we interpret and address contemporary social and political problems.

Rather than being directly translated into behavior, psychologists tell us beliefs can remain latent until "triggered."

In a fascinating study, Karen Stenner shows in *The Authoritarian Dynamic* that while some individuals have "predispositions" towards intolerance, these predispositions require an external stimulus to be transformed into actions. Or, as another scholar puts it: "It's as though some people have a button on their foreheads, and when the button is pushed, they suddenly become intensely focused on defending their in-group … But when they perceive no such threat, their behavior is not unusually intolerant. So the key is to understand what pushes that button."

What pushes that button, Stenner and others find, is group-based threats. In experiments researchers easily shift individuals from indifference, even modest tolerance, to aggressive defenses of their own group by exposing them to such threats. Maureen Craig and Jennifer Richeson, for example, found that simply making white Americans aware that they would soon be a minority increased their propensity to favor their own group and become wary of those outside it. (Similar effects were found among Canadians. Indeed, although this tendency is most dangerous among whites since they are the most powerful group in western societies, researchers have consistently found such propensities in all groups.)

Building on such research, Diana Mutz recently argued that Trump's stress on themes like growing immigration, the power of minorities and the rise of China highlighted status threats and fears particularly among whites without a college education, prompting a "defensive reaction" that was the most important factor in his election. This "defensive reaction" also explains why Trump's post-election racist, xenophobic and sexist statements and reversal of traditional Republican positions on trade and other issues have helped him—they keep threats to whites front and center, provoking anger, fear and a strong desire to protect their own group.

Understanding why Trump found it easy to trigger these reactions requires examining broader changes in American society. In an excellent new book, Uncivil Agreement, Lilliana Mason analyzes perhaps the most important of these: a decades-long process of "social sorting." Mason notes that although racial and religious animosity has been present throughout American history, only recently has it lined up neatly along partisan lines. In the past, the Republican and Democratic parties attracted supporters with different racial, religious, ideological and regional identities, but gradually Republicans became the party of white, evangelical, conservative and rural voters, while the Democrats became associated with non-whites, non-evangelical, liberal and metropolitan voters.

This lining up of identities dramatically changes electoral stakes: previously if your party lost, other parts of your identity were not threatened, but today losing is also a blow to your racial, religious, regional and ideological identity. (Mason cites a study showing that in the week following Obama's 2012 election, Republicans felt sadder than American parents after the Newtown school shooting or Bostonians after the Boston Marathon bombing.) This social sorting has led partisans of both parties to engage in negative stereotyping and even demonization. (One study found less support for "out-group" marriage among partisan Republicans and Democrats than for interracial marriage among Americans overall.)

Once the other party becomes an enemy rather than an opponent, winning becomes more important than the common good and compromise becomes an anathema. Such situations also promote emotional rather than rational evaluations of policies and evidence. Making matters worse, social scientists consistently find that the most committed partisans, those who are the angriest and have the most negative feelings towards out-groups, are the most politically engaged.

What does all this mean for those who oppose Trump and want to fight the dangerous trends his presidency has unleashed?

The short-term goal must be winning elections, and this means not helping Trump rile up his base by activating their sense of "threat" and inflaming the grievances and anger that lead them to rally around him. This will require avoiding the type of "identity politics" that stresses differences and creates a sense of "zero-sum" competition between groups and instead emphasizing common values and interests.

Stenner, for example, notes that "all the available evidence indicates that exposure to difference, talking about difference, and applauding difference … are the surest ways to aggravate [the] intolerant, and to guarantee the increased expression of their predispositions in manifestly intolerant attitudes and behaviors. Paradoxically, then, it would seem that we can best limit intolerance of difference by parading, talking about, and applauding our sameness … Nothing inspires greater tolerance from the intolerant than an abundance of common and unifying beliefs, practices, rituals, institutions and processes."

Relatedly, research suggests that calling people racist when they do not see themselves that way is counterproductive. As noted above, while there surely are true bigots, studies show that not all those who exhibit intolerant behavior harbor extreme racial animus. Moreover, as Stanford psychologist Alana Conner notes, if the goal is to diminish intolerance "telling people they're racist, sexist and xenophobic is going to get you exactly nowhere. It's such a threatening message. One of the things we know from social psychology is when people feel threatened, they can't change, they can't listen."

This has obvious implications for recent debates about civility. Incivility is central to Trump's strategy—it helps him galvanize his supporters by reminding them how "bad" and "threatening" the other side is. Since this has become such a hot-button topic on the left, it is worth being clear what incivility is. There is no definition of democracy that does not accept peaceful protest and other forms of vociferous political engagement. Incivility is about form—not substance; it is consistently defined by scholars as including invective, ridicule, emotionality, histrionics and other forms of personal attacks or norm-defying behavior. By engaging in even superficially similar tactics, Democrats abet Trump's ability to do this—as one Trump supporter put it, every time Democrats attack him "it makes me angry, which causes me to want to defend him more"—potentially alienate wavering Republican-leaning independents, and help divert debate from policies, corruption and other substantive issues.

Of course, there is a double standard here and this, along with the psychic release that comes with venting the anger and grievances that have been building over the past year, are the rationales given by the left for incivility. But against these must be weighed incivility's impact on upcoming elections as well as the overall health of democracy. (Scholars consistently find that incivility spreads rapidly, generates anger and defensive reactions, demobilizes moderates and activates the strongest partisans, corrodes faith in government, trust in institutions and respect for our fellow citizens.)

Over the long term of course the goal is repairing democracy and diminishing intolerance and for this promoting cross-cutting cleavages within civil society and political organizations is absolutely necessary. (Here, recent debates about ideological diversity and the new grassroots activism within the Democratic party is relevant.) Scholars have long recognized the necessity of cross-cutting cleavages to healthy democracy. In his classic study, the Social Requisites of Democracy, Seymour Martin Lipset, for example, noted that "the available evidence suggests that the chances for stable democracy are enhanced to the extent that groups and individuals have a number of cross-cutting, politically relevant affiliations."

More specifically, research has linked cross-cutting cleavages with toleration, moderation and conflict prevention. This too has implications for contemporary debates about "identity politics." Perhaps ironically, identity politics is a both more powerful and efficacious for Republicans (and rightwing populists more generally) than it is for Democrats, since the former are more homogeneous.

As long, therefore, as politics is a fight between clearly bounded identity groups, appeals and threats to group identity will benefit Republicans more than Democrats, which is presumably why Steve Bannon infamously remarked that he couldn't "get enough" of the left's "race-identity politics." "The longer they talk about identity politics, I got 'em ... I want them to talk about race and identity ... every day."

In addition, Americans are more divided socially than they are on the issues; there is significant agreement even on controversial topics like abortion, gun control, immigration and economic policy. Promoting cross-cutting cleavages and diminishing social divisions might therefore help productive policymaking actually occur.

Is our ultimate goal ensuring the compatibility of diversity and democracy? Then promoting the overlapping interests and identifications that enable citizens to become more comfortable with difference and thus more tolerant and trusting, is absolutely necessary.

Periodical and Internet Sources Bibliography

The following articles have been selected to supplement the diverse views presented in this chapter.

Jaden Deal, "Youth Political Engagement and Hope Ahead of the 2020 Election," *Harvard Political Review*, 18 November 2019. https://harvardpolitics.com/united-states/youth-political-engagement-and-hope-ahead-of-the-2020-election/.

Stanley Greenberg, "The Republican Party Is Doomed," *The New York Times*, 10 September 2019. https://www.nytimes.com/2019/09/10/opinion/republicans-democrats-2020-election.html.

Marc Horger, "Breaking up Is Hard to Do: America's Love Affair with the Two-Party System," *Origins*, July 2013. http://origins.osu.edu/article/breaking-hard-do-americas-love-affair-two-party-system.

Robert E. Litan, "America Has Held Together Through Worse Times Than Now," Brookings.edu, 21 February 2018. https://www.brookings.edu/research/america-has-held-together-through-worse-times-than-now/.

Yascha Mounk, "Republicans Don't Understand Democrats—And Democrats Don't Understand Republicans," *The Atlantic,* 23 June 2019. https://www.theatlantic.com/ideas/archive/2019/06/republicans-and-democrats-dont-understand-each-other/592324/.

Jonathan Rauch, "How American Politics Went Insane," *The Atlantic*, July/August 2016. https://www.theatlantic.com/magazine/archive/2016/07/how-american-politics-went-insane/485570/.

Michael Smolens, "Backers of New Political Party Hope 'Common Sense' Prevails," *San Diego Union-Tribune*, 25 September 2019. https://www.sandiegouniontribune.com/columnists/story/2019-09-24/column-backers-of-new-political-party-hope-common-sense-prevails.

Kenneth T. Walsh, "A Familiar Great Divide: One Hundred Years Ago, the Nation and the World Were Divided after World War I. The Same Divisions Are Evident Now," *USNews*, 1 February 2019. https://www.usnews.com/news/the-report/articles/2019-02-01/trumps-divided-america-in-2019-is-similar-to-divisions-in-1919.

For Further Discussion

Chapter 1

1. Where do you think political parties get most of their strength? Why would a strong local organization be crucial to overall success of a political party?
2. Can you see the seeds of today's politics in any of the parties that have come and gone since the founding of the United States? Explain.

Chapter 2

1. How is the system of political parties being more beholden to the wealthy and in some cases actually discouraging the poor and middle classes from voting a type of political corruption?
2. Do you believe that citizen activism can—at least occasionally—influence leaders? Provide examples from your own experience.

Chapter 3

1. Does the disparity between what candidates say during the election and what they do once in office seem to get at the heart of dysfunction in US electoral politics? Why or why not?
2. The viewpoints in this chapter disagree on many particulars, but all argue that the current US political parties are not functioning well. Do you see a pattern in this criticism?

Chapter 4

1. Who serves the role of educating the public about civics and democracy today, and how could this be improved?
2. Why do you think voter turnout is declining, if it is easier than ever to vote? What changes could be made to improve turnout?

Organizations to Contact

The editors have compiled the following list of organizations concerned with the issues debated in this book. The descriptions are derived from materials provided by the organizations. All have publications or information available for interested readers. The list was compiled on the date of publication of the present volume; the information provided here may change. Be aware that many organizations take several weeks or longer to respond to inquiries, so allow as much time as possible.

Cato Institute/Center for Constitutional Studies

1000 Massachusetts Avenue NW
Washington, DC 20001-5403
(202) 842-0200
website: www.cato.org/research/constitutional-studies

The Cato Institute is a think tank that supports limited government, free markets, and peace. It is dedicated to the idea that economic and social freedom are necessary for a free society.

Constitution Party National Committee

PO Box 1782
Lancaster, PA 17608
(800) 283-8647
email: Contactcp@constitutionparty.com
website: www.Constitutionparty.com

The Constitution Party supports candidates who will work to limit the federal government to its enumerate constitutional duties.

Democratic National Committee

430 South Capitol Street SE
Washington, DC 20003
website: www.Democrats.org

The Democratic Party believes that health care is a right, diversity is strength, the economy should work for everyone, and that facts and truth matter.

Democratic Socialists of America

PO Box 1038
New York, NY 10272
See website for contact info for local chapters and field organizers
website: www.dsausa.org

The Democratic Socialists believe that both society and the economy should be run on democratic principles in order to meet the needs of the pubic, not to make a profit for a few.

Generation Citizen

175 Varick Street, 5th Floor
New York, NY 10014
website: www.Generationcitizen.org

Generation Citizen is an organization dedicated to empowering young people to become engaged and effective citizens, by providing them with the knowledge and skills to participate in democracy.

Green Party US

PO Box 75075
Washington, DC 20013
(202) 319-7191
email: office@gp.org
website: www.GP.org

The Green Party supports working people, the Green New Deal, clean water, legal status for immigrants, Medicare for all, women's equality, and a secular, democratic state.

Libertarian National Committee

1444 Duke Street
Alexandria, VA 22314-3403
(800) 353-2887
email: Info@lp.org
website: Lp.org

The Libertarian Party advocates for lowering or eliminating taxes, slashing bureaucracy, ending regulations on business, and charitable rather than government assistance to those in need.

National Democratic Institute

455 Massachusetts Avenue NW
8th Floor
Washington, DC 20001-2621
(202) 728-5500
website: www.Ndi.org

A nonprofit, nonpartisan organization that works to strengthen civic organizations, safeguard elections, and promote citizen participation, openness, and accountability in government.

Republican National Committee

310 First Street, SE
Washington, DC 20003
(202) 863-8500
website: www.GOP.com

The Republican Party believes that the United States should value family life, religious liberty, and hard work, and it works to elect candidates who support those values.

Bibliography of Books

John Avlon. Washington's *Farewell: The Founding Fathers' Warning to Future Generations*. New York, NY: Simon and Schuster, 2017.

Michael Barone. *How America's Political Parties Change (And How They Don't)*. New York, NY: Encounter Books, 2019.

Donna Brazile, Yolanda Caraway, Leah Daughtry, and Minyon Moore (with Veronica Chambers). *For Colored Girls Who Have Considered Politics*. New York, NY: St. Martin's. 2018.

Jessamyn Conrad. *What You Should Know About Politics . . . But Don't*. 4th ed. New York, NY: Arcade, 2019.

Donald T. Critchlow. *American Political History: A Very Short Introduction*. Oxford, UK: Oxford University Press, 2015.

John C. Green, Daniel J. Coffey, and David B. Cohen, eds. *The State of the Parties 2018: The Changing Role of Contemporary American Political Parties*. Lanham, MD: Rowman & Littlefield, 2018.

Jonathan Haidt. *The Righteous Mind: Why Good People Are Divided by Politics and Religion*. New York, NY: Random House, 2012.

Marjorie Randon Hershey. *Party Politics in America*. 17th ed. New York, NY: Routledge, 2017.

Shigeo Hirano and James M. Snyder, Jr. *Primary Elections in the United States*. Cambridge, UK, Cambridge University Press, 2019.

Elaine C. Kamarck. *Primary Politics: Everything You Need to Know About How American Nominates Its Presidential Candidates*. 3rd ed. Washington, DC: Brookings Institute, 2019.

Jill Lapore. *This America: The Case for the Nation*. New York, NY: Liveright, 2019.

Steven Levitsky and Daniel Ziblatt. *How Democracies Die*. New York, NY: Penguin, 2018.

L. Sandy Maisel. *American Political Parties and Elections: A Very Short Introduction*. Oxford, UK: Oxford University Press, 2016.

Steven Pinker. *Enlightenment Now: The Case for Reason, Science, Humanism, and Progress*. New York, NY: Penguin, 2018.

Heather Cox Richardson. *To Make Men Free: A History of the Republican Party*. New York, NY; Basic, 2014.

Katheleen Sears. *American Government 101: From the Continental Congress to the Iowa Caucus, Everything You Need to Know About US Politics*. Avon, MA: F+W Media, 2016.

Kristin Thiel. *Politics and Power in the United States*. New York, NY: Cavendish Square, 2019.

Simone Weil. *On the Abolition of All Political Parties* (NYRB Classic edition). New York, NY: NYRB Classics, 2014.

Index

W

Washington, George, 16, 37

Waskiewicz, Sylvie, 64–71

Watergate scandal, 74

Whig Party, 22, 23, 37–38, 117

winner takes all system, 15, 92, 97, 120

Working Families Party, 91, 93